ONE STEP
AHEAD
of *the* DEVIL

A POWERFUL LOVE STORY

Based on True Events

S.M. HAUSEN

Unless otherwise noted, all Scriptures are taken from the *Holy Bible, New International Version®, NIV®*. Copyright © 1973, 1978, 1984 by Biblica, Inc.™ Used by permission of Zondervan. All rights reserved worldwide. www.zondervan.com

Scripture references marked KJV are taken from the *King James Version* of the Bible.

Scripture references marked NASB are taken from the *New American Standard Bible*, © 1960, 1963, 1968, 1971, 1972, 1973, 1975, 1977 by The Lockman Foundation. Used by permission.

ISBN 13: 9781495355677
ISBN 10: 1495355675
Library of Congress Catalog Card Number: 2011963642

To Bob and Dollie,
with thanks for your encouragement
and support

CONTENTS

INTRODUCTION

RARELY DOES ONE hear about a love this strong! Finding herself in the world of national politics because of David's work, Lissa McCloud faced a modern-day Goliath armed only with her deep faith in God. While David's adversaries were focused on bringing him down, they did not anticipate Lissa's actions. What could a homemaker do anyway? Lissa, a small unassuming young wife was the unexpected factor in this conflict between powerful men. She became the tool God would use to make all the difference. God granted her great courage. He went before her and cleared the way as she battled to save the life of the man she loved.

Based on true events, this amazing love story takes the reader deep into the heart of national politics. Names, descriptions and locations have all been changed to protect the innocent and in order to bring you the full story. Because of the number of people involved, some characters have been combined. But these things really did happen, and God once again demonstrated that he gives strength, courage and an unbeatable spirit to those whose hearts are completely his.

This story will grip both men and women. After listening to the account, one male reporter said, "I have never seen a love like this before!"

PROLOG: DESTINY

MY HUSBAND, DAVID, didn't believe that the dream I kept having was a warning. Not then. Not yet. He was a man of facts and science. He felt my nightmare was a product of trauma I had experienced as a child, and that it meant nothing.

But the dream that haunted me was too precise, too clear, and too consistent for it to be anything but prophetic. I knew in my heart that it was real, that it was a warning of difficult things to come. And in the hours of deep slumber, when my mind was unguarded, it broke across my peace …

The night air was thick and heavy around us. Orange flares sporadically lit the sky. A battle was going on inside the military fort. From our position on the second floor of our home, we could hear the thunder of distant guns. I didn't know where we were, but this was not America. We were on foreign soil.

We crouched together in the dark.

Our two children whimpered, and I held them close.

"You have to get the kids out of here, Lissa!" My husband reached across the children's heads and briefly held my hand. "I'll have to let you down over the fence." He looked toward the window opposite the lights of battle. He disappeared into the bedroom for a moment and returned with a sheet, which he folded several times to create an elongated pad. He leaned out the window and laid it across the barbed wires that topped the security fence. "Come. I'll let you down first, then I'll help the children. Take them to safety."

I threw my arms around him. "Come with us!"

"I can't. I have to stay and help the others fight. Lissa, one of us has to survive this for the sake of the children. It's up to you. Come." He led me to the window.

Gingerly, I climbed over the triple strands of covered barbs and dropped to the ground. I landed on the squishy bank of the jungle swamp. The smell of rotting vegetation filled the air.

Our son, an ash blonde boy of about twelve, placed his feet on the wires above. My husband helped him until I was able to reach up and guide his feet. When our son reached the ground in front of me, my husband lowered our little girl over the fence. She was about eight. Her light brown hair, cut in a short bob, reflected the moonlight.

I looked up for a final glance at the man I loved, who watched from the shadows of the second-story window. The white stucco reflected a burst of orange fire and my husband disappeared into the dark interior of the house. I knew he had gone to join the battle. My heart cried out for him. I could not leave him! But I must. I turned to face the swamp at my feet. It was the only way out of the conflict. "Come, children," I said.

My son started ahead, the swamp water rising to his thighs. Behind me, my little girl froze at the edge of the swamp and cried, "Mommy! Don't leave me!"

I walked back to her. "Climb on my back. I'll carry you, honey."

She wrapped her arms around my shoulders and neck, her feet around my waist. I placed my arms under her legs and stepped out into the swamp alongside my son.

We parted water plants. We dragged our feet out of the mud with each step. I could smell fear in the air. Were there crocodiles? What about water snakes? Through the long night we waded, sometimes slipping on the slime.

Toward morning, I saw an island that rose from the swamp. "Over there," I said softly. I pointed my son toward it with a nod. We climbed out of the swamp and dropped in exhaustion onto the damp ground, falling asleep almost at once.

With the dawn, I opened my eyes and sat up. Through the gloom, I spotted a shale bank at the edge of the swamp—and a hut. A soft light glowed in its window. Behind the hut rose high, blue mountains. Waking the children, I carried my daughter and led my son again into the swamp, moving toward the light.

We walked up the shale bank, and I knocked softly on the door. Our clothes were dripping. Our shoes were soaked.

The door opened and a tall, shadowy man appeared in the hut's dim light. A small group of people stood behind him, craning their necks to see who was at the door. With a calm, low voice, the man said, "Come in."

Americans! They are Americans! I thought with relief.

The people threw blankets around our shoulders and I drew the warm, soft folds around my dripping clothes.

I explained that we were escaping a battle, and that I had to go back to try to get my husband out of it.

"We will watch after your children," the tall man said. "They will be safe with us while you try to help your husband."

I left the cabin and walked back into the swamp. I waded through the murky water all day and into the evening, arriving at the fort by night. I stood outside our home, looked up into the dark room, and called and called. But my husband did not come. Fire lit up the sky in the distance.

"I cannot save him! I cannot save him!" I cried. My hands reached out toward the darkened house … The ground beneath me was shaking … Terror filled my heart … I was drowning in my tears … I heard my name in the distance … It was David's voice.

"Lissa! Lissa, wake up!" David shook my shoulder.

My eyes flew open. David was propped on one elbow, gently shaking my shoulder, looking at me with concern. The soft moonlight detailed the strong muscles of his chest.

"You were having a bad dream," he said.

I moved into his arms, clutching him and wiping tears from my eyes. "It was the nightmare again," I whispered.

I had been plagued by the same dream since childhood. At first I didn't know who the other people in the dream were. It seemed strange to see myself as an adult, a mother with children. But now I recognized two of the people in it: David, my husband, and Ryan, our son. Though Ryan was only a toddler, he had the ash blonde hair of the boy in my dream. Our daughter, Suzanna, had not yet been born. I had told David a little about the dream once before. He did not understand it, but he recognized my terror.

"David, I think it is a prophetic dream. But I don't think God wants me to live in fear. I need you to pray for God to take the dream away. If it is a prophecy, I am warned."

David held me closer and prayed. "Father in heaven, Lissa has had this dream for too long. I ask you to take it away so she will not live in fear any longer. I ask this in Jesus' name, amen."

The dream never returned. Yet it remained vivid in my conscious mind for many years, shaping my choices, shading my future ... haunting me, though it grew fainter with each passing year ... until I rarely remembered it.

TEN YEARS LATER

S UNLIGHT SHIMMERING ON the South China Sea blinded me for
a moment as I stood in the shallows, facing into the wind. "David,
I'm going back to the shade," I called, shielding my eyes.

He waved and smiled, preoccupied with some small creature in the
rocks along the beach. The tide was out. David and our two children,
Ryan and Suzanna, were exploring the necklace of tide pools that adorned
the shore.

I went back to my beach chair under the palm trees to relax, pulling
my long, honey-colored hair to one side and braiding it. Having a fair
complexion, I couldn't take as much sun as my husband and children,
who were blessed with lovely golden skin that seldom burned.

In the distance, a bank of clouds billowed higher. It looked like the
thunderstorm would reach us in about an hour. We still had some time
to enjoy the beach.

Sitting back in my chair, I watched David take some small sea creature
from the pool and place it in Suzanna's cupped hands. Her short brown
hair, recently cut in a page, blew across her face and she shook it away.

I smiled. Suzanna, our eight-year-old, was our unpredictable child.
Led by her heart, she plowed headlong into everything with passion and
determination. I often watched with helpless laughter when she came up
short with unexpected results. Ryan, age twelve, was equally entertained.
We often exchanged amused glances over our darling Suzanna.

David was bending over Suzanna's hands, pointing to the sea creature
she held, no doubt explaining scientific details. Ryan leaned over to see
it, too.

Ryan was our thinker, analytical and thoughtful, yet full of laughter.
He hadn't yet hit the difficult teens, but I could see glimpses of deeper
emotions that would surface. He was a good blend of his father and me,

taking the better characteristics of us both. He had his father's brilliance and my underlying sense of humor. Like David, Ryan was intellectually quick, much stronger-willed than I. He was interested in science and showed indications of wanting to follow in his father's steps.

Yes, David was a great father. He was a natural.

I remembered when we met. We were at a party at a friend's house. The first time David's eyes met mine, he blushed scarlet to the roots of his hair.

His reaction was unusual in Southern California circles. Most of the people I met were sophisticated, even at Biola University, where I worked as an artist. A blush? I hadn't seen one in years.

I was twenty-five, a country girl from Oregon. Though not at all shy, I sometimes felt out of place in the city. My life was simple, practical, open. My family was in the field of medicine, hardworking, well educated, with a love for nature and farm life.

David's blush caught my attention. Maybe he felt as uncomfortable as I did with the fast-paced, complicated society around us. I wondered what he was like. As the party progressed, I noticed he said very little, but his eyes often met mine. David McCloud was a quiet man, yet determined. He found ways to meet me in the days that followed, and little by little he drew me into his world.

He looked like a typical beach boy: light brown hair kissed by the sun, sea green eyes, and a compact, muscular frame. He looked very young, until he grew a mustache. I liked him a lot.

We were surprised to discover we had been attending the same church, First Evangelical Free Church of Fullerton under the leadership of pastor Chuck Swindoll, known for his radio ministry, Insight for Living. The church was huge. Our Sunday school class for single career people numbered over three hundred. David, with his retiring personality, had always stayed in the background.

Shortly after we met, I learned that David wanted to become a doctor. He had already been accepted to medical school. When he told me, I backed away emotionally. I was ready to settle down. Since my family was in medicine, I knew how long and difficult the process of becoming a physician would be. It wasn't for me. We would just be friends.

But David persisted, and I began to fall in love with this quiet, gentle man. I'd never met a man who would stop on the side of the road to rescue birds that had been stunned by cars, or who nurtured wounded animals. His family worked in producing scientific films for use in schools, so he came by this interest in the biological sciences naturally. He was not self-conscious when he was helping an animal ... or a friend. He forgot about himself and concentrated on the need. Only in crowds did he become shy.

He wanted to become a doctor so he could help people in impoverished countries—to be an instrument of God for good, a light where it was needed most.

My own goal was similar. Because my mother died when I was young and my father wasn't sure how to raise me, during my high school years I found myself living in the home of a pastor and his wife. These people, whom I called Mom and Dad, instilled in me a love for mission work. They were my spiritual parents. Because of their influence, I wanted to work with needy children, to teach them about Jesus and help them find a better life through education.

I could feel my resistance weakening the more David expressed what was in his heart. The more we talked, the clearer it became that we belonged together.

Ours was not a wild, passionate relationship, but rather a sweet and strong communion of souls that drew us to each other. When he asked me to marry him, it was inevitable for me to say "yes."

David set aside medical school for a couple years so we could get married and start our family. After medical school, when David was in residency training, we began serious discussions about our future work in a foreign country. We just couldn't agree on *which* country. I was interested in Latin America. David was interested in China, India, and Africa. I used to tease him that his idea of a missionary was someone who wore a pith helmet and carried a machete. "I have nothing against houses with electricity and plumbing!" I told him.

He would laugh and try to convince me the jungle was a great place. I would roll my eyes and laugh, too.

Our relationship had few bumps, for David and I shared similar religious beliefs and values. We both came from working-class families that had struggled to make ends meet. In only one area did we differ: David didn't believe prophecy was for our times, but for ancient days. Yet all my life I had been able to see some events that would happen in the future. Because I had been raised with the same teachings as David, I didn't recognize this was a spiritual gift of prophecy. I didn't understand how it worked, so I said very little about it.

Early in our marriage, I did share with David a brief summary of the prophetic dream that haunted me. I told him I didn't understand what it meant, but that I believed it was some kind of warning. Was the dream symbolic? Or was it a picture of actual events to come? I had long ago decided to take the dream literally, on the off chance that by avoiding the setting, I might be able to prevent the experience. I wanted David to know so he could avoid it too. Some things seemed definite: it would happen on a military base in the tropics, and the battle would begin while we were in a white stucco house. Of this, I felt sure.

My scientific, fact-oriented husband didn't know what to think. Understanding his background, I didn't blame him. He was skeptical, despite my insistence.

I didn't tell him about all the other times God had shown me things before they happened. Like when I was eight and my mother, sister, and brother died. My spirit saw that they were in heaven—before anyone told me they had been killed in a car accident. Or the time I knew a family friend was facing divorce, yet I hadn't seen or spoken to him in eleven years. Or the time I painted a picture of our daughter, Suzanna ... a year before I even met David and seven years before Suzanna was born.

Foreknowledge dotted the landscape of my life. It was an integral part of my being. But I kept it to myself. The churches we attended did not believe in prophetic dreams, and anyone who claimed to have them was viewed with suspicion.

Two weeks after David asked God to take away my nightmare, he announced he had decided to join the army medical scholarship program to help pay for medical school.

I was frantic. "No, David! Remember the dream's warning! The battle in my dream will happen on a military fort!" A rush of fear pulsed through my body. The world seemed to spin. I could barely breathe. "Please, David! Don't do this!"

But David was firm. He felt this was the best way to pay for medical school. To him, my dream was irrelevant. He reasoned with me calmly and allowed me time to think. He was not pushy, but calm and reasonable. His dad had been a tail gunner with General Chennault's Flying Tigers during World War II; military service was held in high regard in his family. Patriotism ran strong in his veins.

When David finally promised he would never ask me to live on a military post, I gave in to his choice—not because I thought he was right, but because I loved him and wanted him to be happy. In our church, I had been taught to respect my husband's leading. Agreeing to his choice, after healthy debate, was what I had been raised to do. In every relationship there had to be a leader, and David was mine. I would go where he led, even if it frightened me. But I wasn't happy about this.

Medical school was long and intense, not just for David but also for me. There was little money, so I did daycare for other families and found ways to make the budget stretch. By the time he finished medical school, David and I had two children, Ryan, age five, and Suzanna, who was one. We moved to the West Coast, where David trained at Letterman Army Medical Center in San Francisco, interning in pediatrics. His medical training gave him a pleasant confidence. Though he was still quiet, he was no longer shy.

A year after he started his training in pediatrics, David recognized that it took him away from our family too much. He changed his specialty to radiology so he would have more time with us. He took an unaccompanied tour to Korea to qualify for the program, leaving me behind with our two young children. Though it was a difficult year for all of us, the result was worthwhile. The radiology program allowed David to take weekends off, and we had much more time together, a welcome relief after the years of medical school.

Four years of specialty training passed quickly. David was now a major, a specialist in radiology. We found ourselves facing a choice: Where would David serve his remaining two years in the military? There were four choices, three in the continental US: Blanchfield Army Community Hospital in Kentucky, Carl R. Damall Army Medical Center in Texas, and Madigan Army Medical Center in Washington. But there was also one overseas opening: Owen Army Hospital on the outskirts of Manila in the Philippines.

David wanted to work in the Philippines. It was the only overseas position available, and he would serve as chief of radiology. In his free time, he wanted to help with local medical missions work. There would also be some opportunities for me. I could explore children's ministries in the city and start making connections with local mission agencies in preparation for future work.

There was only one drawback: In the dream, I had been in the tropics. There had been a swamp with crocodiles and snakes. I hesitated to go to any country where I might be living on a military post *and* living in the tropics.

It had been ten years since I had experienced the prophetic dream, but it still occasionally surfaced in my memory. I was not timid or easily frightened. I tended to be analytical, the result of living with David's scientific approach to life. But this one prophecy, the one that had not yet happened, still scared me.

David had convinced himself, and almost convinced me, that it was not a prophecy at all. Ten years had passed ... yet nothing had happened, so I knew better than to mention the dream as a reason to avoid anything. David would resist any argument based on dreams. I needed to use logic, not fear, in any discussion of the Philippines if I expected David to take me seriously.

"David, we have two children. In the Philippines, they would be exposed to malaria, cholera, typhoid ... How could we fully protect them from those diseases? And there are snakes! I hate snakes, David. It isn't safe for the children there. Besides, I don't do well in hot climates."

He smiled tolerantly. "Lissa, we'll be in the city. The military sprays for mosquitoes on post, and I'm pretty sure the higher-class living areas are sprayed. I doubt there will be any snakes or other wildlife inside the city. The kids will be safe. I'll find us a place with air-conditioning ... off post ... so you won't get overheated. You'll be fine. Come on, Lissa! It will be fun! We can get involved in missions work early this way."

I held out for two months. I was afraid, and I prayed about it a lot. Then one day, I suddenly knew it was okay to go to the Philippines. I felt God's smile on the choice. Peace flooded my heart. At that moment, I knew this was the path God had placed before us, so I yielded to David.

Yes. We would go to the Philippines.

The next day David brought home a big package. I was cooking dinner. The children yelled, "Daddy's home!" and ran to greet him.

I stepped out of the kitchen, a wooden spoon in one hand. "What do you have there?" I asked.

David pulled four pith helmets out of the bag. He put one on his own head, one on each of the children, and one on me. "We're going to be missionaries now," he said solemnly, a twinkle in his eye.

I dissolved into laughter and wrapped my arms around him. He swung me around, laughing with me, while the children watched with puzzled smiles.

We bought a machete in the Philippines and hung it on the wall of David's study ... next to his pith helmet.

Now here I sat on a quiet, sandy beach looking out on the South China Sea, feeling totally at peace, enjoying my family. But my entire world was about to be turned upside-down.

2

THE WHITE STUCCO HOUSE
(APRIL)

T HE AFTERNOON RAIN and a gentle, ocean breeze left the air a little cooler for the party that night. Colonel Lem Aiken, the hospital commander, and his wife, Marge, had invited all the doctors to their house on the hill. The garden was decorated with colorful Chinese lanterns. The flagstone patio was crowded with guests when we arrived. Lively music flooded the air, and couples danced to the beat.

"Lissa!" Marge called, waving over the crowd.

I smiled and waved back with my free hand. My other was clasped firmly in David's as he weaved his way toward our hostess.

"Hi, Marge. Nice party!" I smiled at David as he released my hand. Now that he'd delivered me to Marge, he was looking for her husband. Seeing our host talking with a handful of doctors, David moved away, leaving us to talk.

Marge smiled, her face crinkling into many lines, her faded blonde hair mussed by the breeze. "Good turn-out," she said. "You look like you've had some sun today."

"Yes, we took the children to the beach this morning."

"Would you like something to drink? You must be thirsty."

"Sure. Do you have a ginger ale?"

Marge turned toward the table behind us and drew the ginger ale and a cup of ice. "Here you go."

"Thanks, Marge."

"Say, Lissa, there's a house opening up next door to us. I talked with Lem, and he wants David to move in there."

"Oh!" I was startled.

"I know you've been having a hard time with the heat in the city, and we all have central air-conditioning up here. And it's a lot closer to everything. We can *walk* to the hospital from here! We're all physicians' families, too. And Iris has two kids the same ages as yours." She smiled. "You'd love it here, Lissa."

"Yes, I would," I said slowly. Marge and I had become good friends. I loved her sense of humor. We liked the same things. We even liked the same authors, Agatha Christie and Louis L'Amour ... the latter being an unusual choice for most women. We had fun shopping in town together and lunching with the other doctor's wives.

The houses here were not on a military post. They were near the hospital in a high crime area of the city. But marines patrolled the area. It was most tempting. "I'll talk to David about it."

"Good. Oh, look. There's Nan!" Marge waved.

Nan Barnett, wife of Colonel Barnett, the deputy commander of clinical services, moved gracefully toward us, looking lovely in a red halter dress. Shoulder length black hair glowed in the golden light, and her dark brown eyes sparkled.

Marge reached back to the table and picked up a glass full of white wine. "Here, Nan."

"Thanks." Nan smiled and took a sip. "Did you tell Lissa about the house?"

"Yes. She's thinking about it."

Nan turned to me. "You really should take it, Lissa.'

"I'm thinking." I smiled. I liked Nan a lot, too. Quiet and sweet, she seemed a little shy. From Louisiana, she spoke with a lovely drawl and had exquisite manners. Her children were in high school, with busy lives of their own, so she was looking around for new things to do. Her current project was basket weaving. She lived on Fort Duran, not far from Marge.

While Nan and Marge talked, I looked for David. He was standing with Colonel Aiken, a plain man with a crooked nose from his time in Vietnam. Our host was the life of the party. He was telling a story to the small group of doctors, and David was enjoying it.

Nan's husband, Colonel Barnett, was also in the group. Taller than Colonel Aiken, he had black eyes and his skin was very pale. He was a little socially awkward, and I wondered how he had managed to marry someone as charming as Nan.

I turned back to the two women, listening to their conversation. Yes, it would be nice living closer to them. I'd talk with David about it.

Iris wandered over. Her raven hair, pulled back and held in place with white orchids, gleamed under the lantern lights. "Did you tell her about the house?" she asked Marge.

I laughed. "I've heard!"

"My kids are the only ones on the block. We would *love* to have your kids here, too!"

"Okay. If David likes the idea, we'll do it.

People drifted and regrouped, like the designs in a kaleidoscope, dancing and drinking and talking louder. I found David with Iris's husband, Dr. Lane. They were discussing the health situation in the Philippines, a common topic among the physicians. David was speaking.

"Last weekend I went out to one of the smaller islands with Dr. McMann. You know him?"

"Isn't he the doctor with that medical charity?"

"That's the one. Some islanders met us on the beach and took us out to their village in canoes—with outriggers to handle the waves. The health situation was deplorable. Many of the people build their homes over the water, so there's sewage everywhere."

"I've seen it," Dr. Lane said.

"Then you know what we found. Intestinal parasites, malnutrition, hepatitis, and infected wounds." David shook his head. "It felt like we were barely making a dent in the problems by treating them."

"I know what you mean," Dr. Lane said.

Seeing David deeply involved in conversation, I wandered over to our group and listened to the exploits of Iris' children. After about an hour and a half, David and I made our escape. The alcohol had been flowing freely, and our friends were showing the effects.

On our way home, we talked about the possible move to the hospital neighborhood.

"I like the idea," David said. "I could come home for lunch more often, and I like the idea of central air-conditioning. I think we should take the house."

"Okay," I said. "I think it's a good idea, too."

"I'll put in for it at the housing office tomorrow."

And so it was decided. We would move closer to the hospital.

David's narrative:

Life in the Philippines is very good. We've been here almost a year. For the first time in my life, I feel like I am fulfilling God's purpose, the reason he created me. I enjoy having my own department at the hospital.

When I first arrived, there were tensions between the staff members. Dr. Flores and Dr. Navarro, the two Filipino radiologists working part time, were overwhelmed, trying to run the department themselves. They did not understand the military system, either. The rules confused them. The previous chief of radiology had taken a lot of vacation time and was often away. Work was backlogged. Response time to procedures was between four and five weeks, something I found unacceptable. The staff members, some who were Filipinos, some who were Americans, were at odds with each other.

I'm not good at helping people resolve issues, but I know how classical music can calm an environment. So I brought my stereo system to work and began playing music from Bach, Handel, Schubert, and others. The calm background music brought peace to the ward. Now things are moving smoothly, personnel conflicts have disappeared, and patient reports are completed within two weeks. I feel good about this.

We didn't have any reading material in the lobby at first. Lissa brought some over, but it was immediately stolen. So I called the chaplains and had them set up a reading station, using leftover material from their churches—things people were welcome to take. It's working well. The chaplains are using the station as a means of getting Bibles into the hands of the Filipino people. I like what they're doing.

Last weekend I went to one of the more primitive islands with a civilian friend, Dr. McMann, to hold a medical clinic. Dr. McMann works with a US-based medical charity. We spent the weekend dispensing medicine and treating wounds and infections. There were a lot of medical needs. This was our second trip to the outlying islands, and I can see that I'll have to do more study into tropical illnesses to be more effective. There is much to learn. We're planning another medical trip next month.

Lissa was home-schooling the children this year, so I hired a maid to help her around the house. Her name is Marina. She has a ten-month-old baby. Lissa didn't want her traveling across the city every day with the child, so Marina and her baby live with us. I'm glad I could provide this extra household help, and it seems to be working well. Lissa and Marina have become the best of friends.

When Lissa told me about the house next door to Colonel Aiken, I liked the idea. It is close to the hospital, and it is only two blocks from the radio station where Lissa is doing a weekly children's program. It would have been convenient.

But there has been a hitch. Yesterday the housing office called and offered a choice of two houses on post. Some colonel was assigned to the house next to Colonel Aiken. Now I have to break the news to Lissa. She isn't going to like it. She has a deep fear of living on a military post. The alternative is to stay where we are, but I cannot let her continue suffering in this heat. Every day when I come home, I find her limp with exhaustion. We both have trouble sleeping at night in this heat. We need a good air-conditioner, and we'll be able to get that on post.

When my time with the Army Medical Corps is finished next year, we'll probably move to a cooler part of the world. We've been thinking about Quito, Ecuador. There's a mission hospital next to a Christian and Missionary Alliance school and a Christian radio station. I've been in touch with the hospital, and we're thinking of taking a trip there during my next vacation. Lissa speaks Spanish, so she'll probably love it.

But for now, I'm enjoying this experience of working in the Philippines. I just hope Lissa is willing to live on post at Fort Duran.

The thunderstorm crashed around our car. The air-conditioning was blowing full blast to keep the windshield free of steam as the wipers whipped at the highest speed. We were traveling home from an outing in the mountains.

I sat in silence trying to absorb what David had just said. He asked me to live on post! I could not believe it. When I agreed to his joining the military, he promised he would never ask me to do that. Now we were in the military, in the tropics, and he wanted to move our family into the very setting I had feared! My heart pounded in unison with the wipers.

"Well?" David said.

"Let's talk about it later." I needed time to think. I stared out the window, not seeing the darkening jungle around us. We would be home in a little while. I didn't want to discuss it in front of the children.

I would have liked living next to the hospital, where David would have been five minutes away. Marge would have been next door, Iris across the street, and Nan just a couple blocks away.

The small American community was close-knit. Because we lived off post that first year, I was not part of most of the social life, yet I was on good terms with the other wives. Still, the idea of living on post frightened me.

Sitting stiffly next to David, I decided to ask God what he wanted of me before responding to David's suggestion. Gradually, I felt the tension and fear drain away. When we arrived home, I went up to our bedroom. Sitting on the balcony overlooking the city, I considered what we would need in a house if we were to move on post.

"Father in heaven, I need to know if you are in this plan of David's! Living on a military post in the tropics ... Lord! Is this your plan for us? I need to have some solid assurance of your approval before I agree to this." I sat quietly for a few minutes, willing my heart to listen for impressions. Then something came: I should list what I would like to have if we were to live on post. If God provided everything on the list, I would be sure he was behind the move. I asked for:

1) A house with maid quarters for Marina and the baby
2) Three bedrooms for the family
3) A house on a cul-de-sac where the children could ride their bikes safely
4) A big lawn where the children could play
5) Tall trees around the house and lawn to protect us from the tropical heat
6) A place for David to park his boat

My heart was at peace after I made the list. I folded it and put it in my pocket.

The next day I told David, "Honey, I will look at the houses with you, but I'm not promising anything." It was late Sunday afternoon. I felt calm, open to God's leading, and sure he would guide us.

"Okay. Let's go right now," David said. "I don't want to miss this opportunity. If we don't choose quickly, someone else will get the houses that are available. Who knows how long we'll have to wait for another opening."

We drove to Fort Duran. The first house was a simple three-bedroom, with no place for Marina and Rosy. It was located on a busy street. I took one look and shook my head.

"Okay. Let's go see the other house."

We drove across the fort to the second listing, and there it stood: a tall, white stucco duplex, with maid quarters on the bottom level. It had three bedrooms. It was on a street ending with a cul-de-sac. There was a huge lawn behind it, and tall shade trees. There was even a slab for parking David's boat! I learned later that it was the *only* house with boat parking on the entire fort. It had originally been the house of the base building contractor, and he had poured the concrete for his own boat.

I laughed.

David looked at me. "What's so funny?"

I handed him my list. "I told God that if he provided all these things, I would know it was his will for us to move on post."

David read the list and grinned. "I guess that means I can tell the housing office we'll take this house."

And so he did.

It didn't register that this might be the house in my nightmare. Everything had been dark in the dream, with orange lights flickering on the stucco walls. By daylight, this house looked different. In the dream, there was a security fence next to the house. But here, the fence stood at the end of the street. Beyond the security fence was the jungle.

I did not realize that dreams telescoped things together. If I had recognized the setting, nothing could have made me move on post. In that moment, all I could see was that this house had all the requirements I had asked God to provide as a sign of his blessing, and he had done so. It was enough.

3

THE FIRST SKIRMISH
(JUNE)

Owen Army Hospital Command Structure

Colonel Lem Aiken, M.D.
Commander
(Reports to oversight general at Tripler AMC, Hawaii,
and to Gen. Neil, Ft. Duran)

Colonel Barnett, M.D. (DCCS)
Deputy Commander, Clinical
Services
(All medical department chiefs
report to DCCS)

Colonel Calloway (DCA)
Deputy Commander,
Administration
(All administrative department
chiefs report to DCA)

Major David McCloud, M.D.
Chief of Radiology
  Staff: Dr. Navarro, radiologist
  Dr. Flores, radiologist
  All radiology technicians
  Candy Reyes, office manager
  Clerical staff

Note: Department chiefs were supposed to be Army Medical Corps physicians. But due to the shortage of personnel, some Filipino doctors were serving as "acting department chiefs" while awaiting the assignment of AMC physicians.

"LISSA, LET'S GO for a walk," David said after dinner about a month after we moved on post. We usually waited until the children were in bed before we walked around the fort's manicured grounds. I could tell something was bothering him.

"Sure. Let me get my walking shoes." I was used to listening to David's concerns about patient care. Had he done the right thing? Would the patient be okay? He was a physician; he dealt with life and death. I knew little about medicine, but I knew it helped him to talk things out, though he never told me patient names or personal matters. Patient privacy was part of medical rules, even then. But I could pray about his work and his unnamed patients.

Three minutes later, I took David's hand as we walked into the twilight. I breathed in the scent of rain-washed lawns and hibiscus flowers, enjoying the moment. I loved living on post! The central air-conditioning kept the house cool, and I had revived from the year of toughing it out in the city.

Across the street from us lived Mark and Julie, who had just started their family. Mark was a major, like David. He had recently worked as an inspector general officer, but was now working as an adviser to a colonel in the finance department. Julie was pulling groceries from her car, and she smiled as we walked by. I waved and smiled back.

Around the corner lived Colonel Calloway, the deputy commander of administration at Owen Army Hospital, and his wife Mary. They were moving back to the States at the end of the week. In the short time we had been neighbors, I had come to enjoy Mary's company. I knew I would miss her. Mary and her husband had a son the same age as Ryan. The two boys had been tossing a football around on the huge lawn behind our house, and exploring the neighborhood. I hadn't realized how much I'd missed English-speaking neighbors until we moved on post.

The daily rain had passed, but the sky remained overcast and the air was muggy. Streetlights lined the sidewalk, and a slow-moving truck sprayed for mosquitoes on a cross street. It was far enough away that it didn't drown the delicate perfume of the hibiscus flowers along our path.

"Something happened at work today," David said. "Colonel Barnett handed me a pile of Filipino physicians' time cards, some that were three years old—from the years before I arrived. The stack was between one-and-a-half and two inches high. Colonel Barnett told me to alter them. He's been keeping two sets of time records. The radiologist before me hired the local doctors to work longer hours than the army allowed. One of the doctors wasn't even properly approved. Colonel Barnett paid them for half the time they worked … the time that was allowed by the army. Now he wants me to say they served those extra hours on my watch, which they didn't. The amount of money involved is huge! I can't do this, Lissa. It's fraud."

Oh, this was not about life and death. It was about hospital politics. That made it easier. David was the most diplomatic person I'd ever met, so I felt he would find a way to handle the problem.

"What did you say to him?" I asked.

"I didn't say anything. I was too surprised." So far, all David's coworkers in the army had been men and women of honor and integrity, both at Letterman Army Medical Center and in Korea, where he had spent a year at the 4077th M.A.S.H., the unit on which the television series was based. This was David's first contact with corruption in the military. He had not expected it.

"I showed the time cards to Candy, my office manager, and she said Colonel Aiken and Colonel Barnett both tried to get her to alter time cards before I came here, and she held out for a long time. She is a highly trained Filipino, and she has been trained in army protocol and regulations. She said the commander hounded her to sign the cards until she nearly had a nervous breakdown. She told me this was fraud, and advised me not to sign those cards."

I didn't know what to say, but I was only moderately concerned. David would find a way to fix this. He always found a way. I just needed to let him talk it out.

"When I first arrived, Colonel Aiken himself wrote a hospital-wide memo stating this practice of time card alteration was illegal! I looked up the regulation, and it states that only an officer with the rank of colonel or the civilian equivalent can grant permission and sign for overtime not approved by the military. I'm just a major. But Colonel Barnett wants *me* to alter and sign those time cards. If he is so insistent on this issue, why doesn't he take the responsibility for it? It's his job!"

Now I was starting to see the problem. Something fishy was going on.

"The lawyers at Letterman warned me about this practice before I left for this assignment. They said it was illegal, and that under the new laws Congress passed against waste, fraud, and abuse, anyone caught doing this sort of thing would be prosecuted ... and that if anyone learns about waste, fraud, or abuse, they must report it to the inspector general or they, too, will be prosecuted. It's a sensitive subject because this practice has been going on for a long time. The military high command is determined to stamp it out, and they're actively going after it."

"What are you going to do?" A breeze shook a cluster of raindrops from the tree overhead, and the water ran down the back of my neck. I shivered and tugged at my blouse.

David shrugged. "I will not sign them."

We walked in silence for a few minutes. Finally, David reached a conclusion.

"I will point out to Colonel Barnett that his own signature is on some of those cards. Since this happened before I arrived, he should be the one to authorize pay for those doctors. I will tell him that I feel uncomfortable altering time cards."

That *might* work, I thought. This whole situation felt wrong. It seemed there was something else beneath the surface, something neither David nor I knew about.

We walked silently around the post at a faster pace than usual. I could sense the struggle in David's heart. He would occasionally comment on the situation and wonder aloud how to handle it.

Forty-five minutes later, I followed David up the hill toward our home. The streetlight was flickering. It cast a sporadic orange glow against the white stucco. I hesitated, staring at the house. It looked uncannily familiar.

A foreboding began to creep over me. I hurried and caught up with David at the top of the stairs. He opened the door for me and I walked past him and up the stairs to our bedroom. Showering quickly and donning jeans and a peasant blouse, I hesitated by the window, looking into the night at the display of lights across the fort, wanting a few minutes alone to think. But hearing the children laughing in the living room, I knew I needed to rejoin the family. I took a deep breath and went back downstairs.

"Mommy! Look at this funny picture of Ryan!" Suzanna pointed to the photo album on her lap. I sat down next to her and looked over her shoulder.

Ryan and David were wrestling on the floor.

"Let me see!" Ryan broke free of David's grip and reached for the album.

"I'm holding it!" Suzanna grabbed the top of the album and leaned over it.

Ryan plopped on the couch next to her. "Okay, you can hold it. But let me see!"

The page held Halloween pictures of Ryan at age four, the year Suzanna had been born. Ryan was a lion that year and Bethany, his friend, was a pony. They looked adorable. I smiled, remembering the feel of the yellow flannel the day I made the costume, the soft, rosy cheeks of my son and the glow in his eyes when he looked at himself in the mirror, his face framed with a golden mane of yarn.

I looked across the room at David. He had walked to the window and was staring into the night, his shoulders stiff, hands in his pockets. Tension returned to my heart. He had only one more year to serve before he could leave the army.

Now I began to wonder: Would we make it out okay? I took a deep breath and turned my heart toward trust in God. There was no point in worrying. We could face tomorrow when tomorrow arrived.

The week continued. David said nothing more about the incident, and I relaxed. The children's activities, fixing meals, shopping, my new job in broadcasting at the Christian radio station, and church claimed my attention. Everything drifted back to normal.

But the problem had not disappeared. A week later, during our evening walk, David said, "Colonel Barnett came to my office today and asked me if I'd finished altering the time cards. I told him I was uncomfortable with his request, since the judge advocate general [JAG] at Letterman had told me this practice was illegal." He fell silent.

"David? What did he say?"

"He became very angry. He ordered me to sign them. I told him I needed to talk to the JAG first."

We walked in silence. I could see that David was struggling to work this out.

"I've made an appointment at JAG for tomorrow morning," he said. "Maybe they can help with the situation."

I felt cautiously optimistic. Surely we could trust the JAG.

David's narrative:

I made an appointment with Colonel Marcus, the chief of JAG. When I reached his office, I saw a colonel standing inside, looking through files. I said, "Colonel Marcus?"

He turned and looked at me, then walked past me as though he hadn't seen me. His nametag read "Marcus." Why didn't he speak? Why did he walk away?

I stepped into the hall and watched him walk outside. Puzzled, I looked around. There was another JAG officer coming toward me, a major. He asked if he could help me.

"Yes, I have an appointment with Colonel Marcus."

The JAG officer looked uncomfortable. "May I help you instead?"

So I went into his office to discuss the time card situation. He asked if the Filipino doctors had worked those hours. When I confirmed that they had, he said, "Well, then we need to pay them. Go ahead and sign the time cards." But he wouldn't look me in the eye.

I told him, "Since this is an irregular situation, I will need a written statement from you saying an exception has been granted for this reimbursement."

The JAG officer shook his head. "No. Just go ahead and sign the cards. We don't want to make a big deal about it."

Something smells wrong about this whole business. I won't sign those cards without written authorization from either the JAG or my commanding officer, and neither is willing to give that. I need some legal advice from someone outside the situation.

That evening when David returned from work, I was in the kitchen finishing the meal. He leaned against the doorway and told me what had happened at JAG.

"I don't like it, David." I shook my head.

A frown touched his brow. "I need to talk to Brian Newall."

"Isn't he the lawyer we had over to dinner before we left San Francisco?"

"Yes. He's the JAG officer I met in Korea. We were both attending a Korean church in town, and he's a solid Christian. His next assignment was here at Owen Army Hospital. He left here a month before we came. He knows the situation."

"Where is he now?"

"He's in California. I've got his office number." David looked at his watch and calculated. "It's Friday. I'll wait until tomorrow morning and call him at five o'clock. It will be four o'clock Friday afternoon where he is."

The next morning I sat up in bed and listened while David dialed Brian.

"Brian? This is David McCloud."

I could hear a deep voice coming over the phone as Brian spoke. His words came through clearly.

"David! What are you doing? Aren't you in the Philippines?"

"Yes, I'm at Owen Army Hospital."

"That's what I thought. How's the family?"

"We're good. Hey, Brian, I need some legal advice."

"Uh-oh. What'd you do?"

"Nothing yet."

"Okay. Don't keep me in suspense."

"The commander and deputy commander have ordered me to alter some time cards for the Filipino doctors who work here."

"Don't do it. You are not required to follow an illegal order, you know. I hope you refused!"

"I did. Now they're upset at me. What should I do?"

"Hold your ground, brother. I know those men. The commander has a reputation for being a cowboy. He has been investigated many times by the inspector general [IG], but his commanding officers have always let him off the hook. There was an IG investigation on time card fraud just last year. Someone stole the report from the JAG office! We never found it or figured out who had taken it, and the commander managed to smooth things over. But the IG is onto him. They're watching pretty close. Don't get mixed up in this, Dave. It's cause for court-martial."

David sighed. "Okay. I'll hold firm."

"Dave, you need to make photocopies of those time cards and hold onto them. Document every conversation with your commanding officers immediately afterward. Record the date and time of each conversation. They're called 'notes of memorandum,' and the records are accepted as legal documents, should this lead to legal action. In fact, you should probably put all your responses to your commander on this subject in writing." He paused. "David?"

"Yes?"

"This commander has a habit of calling the JAG office and pressuring people to do what he wants. I don't know what he says, but I've wondered if he is putting undue pressure on someone in command at JAG. You know what I mean?"

"I understand. Anything else?"

"No. Just be careful. How's the family?"

They talked for a few minutes, then David hung up and looked at me.

"I heard. You have to hold your ground."

"I know." He walked to the bedroom window and looked out. The sun was beginning to drop below the tops of the trees. In a moment it would disappear. "This isn't going to be easy, Lissa. I'll need your help. I can't make photocopies of those time cards at work. You'll have to find a photocopier in town and do that for me."

"I know of a place where there's one. Bring the time cards home and I'll do it."

4

MAMBABARANG

David's narrative:

It has been two weeks since I told Colonel Barnett I would not sign fraudulent time cards. Colonel Aiken has called me into his office many times since that day. He and Colonel Barnett have taken turns trying to harass me into signing those cards. Their approach has been manipulative and undermining.

The first day, they told me, "David, you are a troubled man. You work too hard! You are too quiet. Who are your friends? You keep to yourself and aren't one of the guys. We think you need some professional help. And by the way, you should sign those time cards and trust us on this."

That has been the general theme of their hour-long harangues. They have harped on this same topic in each session, each time pointing out some failing they see in me, insinuating I'm mentally ill! They call me away from work two or three times some days and keep me for at least an hour. I've missed upwards of eighteen hours of work in the past two weeks. I'm getting behind and have to work late to catch up.

No, I do not "hang out with the guys" after work. My world is my family, my Christian friends, and mission trips to help people who are in need. I don't enjoy going to the officer's club and getting drunk with the other doctors. It isn't my thing.

They've been sending me to the drug-testing lab two or three times a week, too, and the personnel there make comments like, "We didn't catch you this time. But we will!"

I don't do drugs! What are they hoping to gain from this harassment?

This is getting old. But I will not sign those time cards. I have shared my faith in Christ with my staff. What would it say about my trust in God if I were to fail at the first testing of my faith? The apostle Peter instructed Christians about how to handle these things when he said, "It is better, if it is God's will, to suffer for doing good than for doing evil."[1] That is what I must keep in focus.

I believe Colonel Aiken and Colonel Barnett intend to use psychiatric retaliation against me to try to force me to do their dirty work, since my supposed mental needs are the focus of their harassment.

This seems like such a stupid thing to fight over! Time cards? What are they thinking! Since they need to pay the Filipino doctors, why doesn't the commander take responsibility, go to the JAG, and make arrangements legally?

I'm not sure how this is going to work out, but I am putting my trust in God. That's all I can do.

I WATCHED ANXIOUSLY as David began working long hours. He started complaining of severe headaches. I didn't wonder, considering the pressure he was under. He wouldn't tell me any details of what was happening at work. He's a "headline" communicator. He merely said, "I think my commanding officers are planning to use psychiatric retaliation against me."

How could these officers, who claimed to be our friends, turn on David like this?

One evening I asked Marina about something I'd overheard at the hospital that afternoon. We were making dinner together at the time.

"Marina, what is *mambabarang?*" My understanding of the local language was improving, but I didn't know that word.

Marina nearly dropped the kettle of spaghetti she was taking to the sink. She looked at me seriously. "I don't know your word for this. It is peoples who ask bad spirits to hurt other peoples. They have beetles that are devils that they send to attack others, then the other people get sick. Sometimes they die! *Mambabarangs* make dolls and put pins in them. There are some very bad ones on island of Siquijor. Some *mambabarangs* move to here for more work."

I stirred the spaghetti sauce. "Today I overheard someone at the hospital talking about hiring a *mambabarang.* They shut up when they saw me and hurried away."

"Miz Lissa," Marina said, "you must be very careful! I hear you and Doctor David talking about problems at Owen Army Hospital. It is bad there. I have friend whose husband tell inspector general about bad peoples who work there. When trial come, *mambabarang* stay in hallway and chant and do witch powder and doll with needles in it. My friend's husband became very sick and had to go to hospital. He died! Many peoples hire the *mambabarang* when they have problems with others. Dr. David must be careful, please!"

I discussed it with David later that evening. He wasn't worried. He thought witch doctors were only for the superstitious, and they couldn't affect him.

Morning after morning, Colonel Aiken and Colonel Barnett pounded away at David, trying to force him to cooperate with their illegal scheme and taking him away from his work for long periods.

He didn't yield, and the tension escalated.

After the third week, Colonel Aiken warned David he would be in danger from the Filipinos if he continued to hold out on the time cards. Indeed, the Filipino doctors had become unfriendly and angry toward David. Colonel Aiken had obviously been telling them David was the one responsible for holding back their pay.

David's hours grew longer as he tried to keep up with his work under the continually interrupted schedule. I became more concerned about him. I wondered if his health could take that pressure.

One evening, he came home very late and went straight to bed, complaining of a headache. A few hours later he awoke. "Lissa." His voice was strained. "I can't move."

"What is it, honey?" I sat up in bed.

"My heart is racing. I'm having tachycardia!"

"What's that?" I asked, alarmed.

He struggled to catch his breath. "It's when the heart races for several seconds. It's done that a couple times now. And I feel like my body is too heavy to lift."

"Let's go to the hospital!"

"No! I don't trust those doctors."

"David, you *must* see a doctor!"

"I'm afraid!" David whispered. "This evening I had a cup of black coffee to stay awake at work. I was in and out of the office and only had time to finish half the cup. When I was getting ready to leave, I noticed a whitish scum on the surface of the coffee, so I threw it out. Now I'm feeling weird—like what I've read about amphetamine overdoses. I will not go to that hospital for treatment!"

David made it through the night and called in sick the next morning. He was still feeling weak. I finally convinced him to come with me to the emergency room.

The Filipino doctor was cold and abrupt. He drew blood for testing and sent David home.

Later that day, when Marina and I were baking mango cookies, I told her about David's tachycardia, the coffee that may have had something in it, and all the harassing drug tests.

"It sounds like *mambabarang!*" Marina looked troubled. "I have seen this before. Sometimes people buy powder from *mambabarang* to give to their enemies."

I pulled a tray of cookies from the oven and set them on a cooling rack.

"Miz Lissa," Marina said, "This colonel has done this kind of thing before, making problems for good people who want to do right thing. He is very bad man. I have very good friend. I name my baby after her. Rosy's husband work at Owen Army Hospital. He is a sergeant. His name is Allen Matthews. Allen and one of his men go to the hospital in Manila to take a patient from Owen hospital to there. He see many things at that hospital that belong to Owen Army Hospital. Things they should not have. He and his man report this to inspector general. A week later, both men are told to take drug test. Both are said to have cocaine! But he is family man and he doesn't use drugs. He and the other man have to leave army."

"Marina, do you know how I can reach Allen?"

"Yes. I have phone number."

"Thank you, Marina. You are such a help to me! If you will go get his phone number, I'll call him after we're finished baking cookies."

Marina hurried downstairs to to hunt for the information while I scrubbed potatoes for dinner. The oven timer buzzed. The cookies were done. Marina came back into the room, handed me a slip of paper, then began peeling the potatoes.

I glanced at the paper. Allen Matthews was living in Maui, working in the civilian world. I reached for the kitchen phone.

"Mr. Matthews? My name is Lissa McCloud. I'm calling from the Philippines. My maid, Marina, said I should talk to you."

I told him about David's situation. I had barely finished when he burst into words.

"Yes! Colonel Aiken does that sort of thing!" he said. "I saw equipment from Owen Army Hospital in a Manila hospital. Lots of it. The private who was with me saw it too. We told the hospital IG. A week later, we both faced drug charges for cocaine use! But neither of us used cocaine. When it came time for trial, I demanded a DNA test on their sample, but the lab guy said he'd lost the evidence!

"The guy in the lab was caught using cocaine the year before," Allen said, "but Colonel Aiken kept him on. I think the lab tech owes the colonel a few favors and is being used. Anyway, there was no evidence against either the private or me. But the military chose to discharge us. They gave us both *honorable* discharges!"

Could this be real? It seemed unbelievable! "Thank you, Allen. That information helps."

"Glad I could help. Good luck! And tell Marina that Rosy is well and that we're expecting a baby in two months."

"I'll pass that along." I hung up the phone and stood staring into space, trying to process this information.

My mind went back to what David had told me. Colonel Aiken had warned him that he would be in danger from the Filipinos. Might there really have been drugs in that cup? If David had finished that coffee, would he still be alive?

I went to the bedroom and told David about Allen.

He was silent and grim.

"David, I don't know what's happening, but we're a long way from home, and I'm scared."

"I am too, Lissa." David reached for my hand. "So let's pray." He bowed his head and laid the problem before God.

I sighed. I fixed a cup of tea, then sank into the couch. My mind raced. What could I do?

David, like most men, wouldn't think of asking for help. Yet he needed someone in higher command to help him. I grew up with conflict around me, and I understood this colonel. I had spent some time trying to cope with people like him. It was like walking on eggshells, hoping in vain that nothing would break. Some people are such egoists, they can tolerate no opposition, no matter how small. If they do not get their own will, down to the tiniest detail, they destroy the one standing in the way. But David didn't understand that; nothing in his life had prepared him to deal with people like that.

From what Brian and Allen had said, Colonel Aiken was such a man. He would use his position of power to seriously hurt my husband, for David would not yield to fraud, threats, or coercion. Though David was quiet, he could not be pushed. He was a man of honor.

But his colonel was not. He was drunk on power.

Colonel Barnett? Why was he involved? Maybe he had just been swept into the situation. Or maybe this was the old way of doing things, and he felt it was the right way, regardless of the new laws. Doctors who make decisions every day on matters of life and death tend to think they are above the law.

David was no match for this evil. I had to do something to help him. The threats, followed by the tachycardia, were serious. David was not the kind to ask for help. But what could I do? In the eyes of the military, I was "just a wife," a woman in a man's world. An officer's wife was nothing more than a decoration to enhance her husband's career. I had no standing.

It was time to bring David's parents into this. We needed prayer! Late that night, I put a call through and filled them in. "Please, Mom and Dad, pray for us!"

"You know we will!"

"Thanks. We know that God is bigger than this problem." I felt sure that—with two solid prayer warriors backing us up—things would change.

APPEAL FOR HELP

Military Command Structure		
(only those involved in this account)		
Admiral Grady, Pacific Command Commander-in-Chief		
Over all military facilities/operations in Pacific Command (PACCOM) Member of the Joint Chiefs, reporting to President of the United States		
Colonel Farr Inspector General Philippines (Navy)		**Colonel Erickson** Marine Commander Philippines
General Neil, Commanding General		
Fort Duran (Army) (All Army commanders report to Gen. Neil)		
Colonel Aiken, M.D. Hospital commander (Army)	**Colonel Duffy, M.D.** Surgeon Gen., Philippines (Army)	**Colonel Marcus** JAG Commander Philippines (Army)

ARLY DAWN TOUCHED the sky, and I could hear the children moving upstairs. David had managed to drag himself out of bed and had returned to work.

With the children awake, my quiet time with the Lord was over. I rose and closed my Bible. After the tachycardia incident, I was terribly frightened for David's life. Setting my empty cup in the kitchen, I considered my plan. What was the value of living on post if we couldn't appeal to the fort's commanding general? Surely he could help us.

The children clattered downstairs for breakfast. As soon as they finished eating and dashed outside to play, I put my plan into action. I changed into a dress and braided my hair.

Too nervous to eat much, I drank another cup of tea and had a piece of toast.

"Marina," I said, "I'm going over to headquarters to speak with the general. Wish me well."

"Yes, Miz Lissa. I will pray for you!" Marina said. We had become close over the past few months. We cooked and laughed and talked together, and I often took her along when I traveled into the city. Of all the people I'd met, Marina was my dearest friend in the Philippines. She was like a sister.

Palm trees, hibiscus, and close-cut lawns lined the sidewalks that led to the command center, with its red tiled roofs and white stucco walls. The sky was clouding up with the promise of rain. The air was sticky.

It took only a few minutes to reach headquarters. I brushed my hands on my skirt to rub the moisture from my palms and breathed a prayer. I walked up the red brick steps and opened the door to the main office. I looked for the general's office. The door to his aide's office stood open, so I hesitantly entered.

"I'd like to see General Neil, please."

She looked startled.

"Please have a seat, Mrs …?"

"Mrs. McCloud."

"What should I tell the general you wish to see him about?"

"My husband is Dr. David McCloud. He works at Owen Army Hospital and is facing some serious problems. I know it is not my place to intervene, but something bad just happened. We need the general's help."

"Just a moment," she said. "I will see if General Neil will see you." She disappeared through the door to the general's office and shut it behind her.

I sat in a straight-backed chair and looked around the office. It was stark, with a battered, wooden desk for the aide. The floor was hardwood. The walls were painted cream, and there were no decorations. It was a very old building, smelling slightly of mold.

The aide returned and apologetically informed me that General Neil would not see me, but that he had asked her to take my information.

Good enough. I laid the entire problem before the aide. She looked shocked. She turned and disappeared into the general's office. This time she was gone quite a while. When she returned, she asked, "What do you want General Neil to do for you?"

"I want General Neil to protect my husband."

That night, when David and I were alone, I told him what I'd done.

He was electrified by my boldness. "Lissa, this is the *army!* You can't do things like that! You might get me into trouble!"

I didn't flinch. I knew David would react like that.

But I was a fighter. What I had done was a good strategic move, proper protocol or not.

I brushed my hair and slipped into bed while David paced the room. He would eventually settle down. I was untroubled by his nervousness. If I knew anything about men, I knew they usually respond to appeals for help from women, and General Neil was no different than any other man.

David had physical training (PT) the next morning, something he did every other morning. All officers were supposed to participate in PT three times a week, but few of the doctors did. David was an exception. He enjoyed the early morning run and the exercise.

That morning when he returned from PT to shower and change for work, David's eyes were glowing. "Guess who showed up at PT this morning?"

"Who?"

"General Neil!" He was pumped.

I laughed.

"Colonel Aiken and Colonel Barnett usually show up for roll call at PT, then they leave. But they had to stay this time because of the general. Everyone was alert and excited, because the general rarely comes to PT.

"He led the troops on the morning run," David said. "Once we were started, he elbowed his way back to where I was, and he ran next to me the whole time!"

"Wow!" I was catching David's excitement.

"When I got to work, Colonel Aiken called me into his office … again. He was very angry. He asked, 'How did General Neil hear about this? Who are your friends?' I didn't answer him. Colonel Aiken finally said, 'General Neil sent a message to me this morning by running with you … that you are to be left alone!'"

David sighed. "I think things should start to settle down now."

"You mean that's *it?* The general didn't *say* anything?"

"No. That's how things are done in the military. Nobody wants to go on record. So they do things like this to send messages to others. It allows them to claim plausible deniability in the event of an investigation. Crazy, isn't it?"

I shook my head. To me, it sounded cowardly. Oh, well. General Neil had stood up for David in his own way, and that was what mattered. I was grateful. David now had a powerful protector.

But just how committed was the general?

It was Friday and I had joined the other doctors' wives for lunch at the officer's club on the hill overlooking the fort. There were five of us: Marge, Nan, Iris, Megan, and I. Megan, a cute young redhead, was new to our group. Her husband, Dr. Weber, was chief of pediatrics.

Marge had reserved a corner table. Sunlight shone on the banana plants and palm trees outside, and our corner was bathed in a pleasant glow.

Marge, sitting at the corner next to me, tapped me on the arm. "You won't believe what Betty Delaney told me!" she said, loud enough for the others to hear.

"What?" Iris asked.

"You know how that new colonel has been hitting on every woman at the club? Well ..." Marge took off on a scandalous, probably highly imaginative account of what had happened between Betty Delaney, the young, beautiful captain from the transportation department, and the colonel.

I only half-listened to the story, smiling when I heard the others laugh. Did these women know what was going on at the hospital? Did Marge and Nan know about the pressure their husbands were putting on mine?

"Lissa." Marge tapped my arm again. "Where are you?"

I laughed and returned my focus to the group. "Sorry. I was thinking about something else. Nothing important."

"So, do you want to come with us?"

"Well, it depends." I had no idea what she was talking about! My mind had been caught up in David's struggle.

"Oh, you should come!" Megan said. "There's a new shop on the strip that's selling native crafts. Iris says it's new. You have to see it, Lissa."

"We're leaving from my place at nine o'clock Tuesday morning," Marge said. We'll go shopping first, then we'll come back here for lunch."

"I'm sorry. I don't think I can go on Tuesday," I said, relieved that there was a conflict on my schedule. "I have to do my children's radio program that morning."

Marge looked at me in blank surprise. "What children's program?"

"I do a music program for the English-speaking children every week. It's just children's songs and a story. On Tuesday, I record it. Then the station broadcasts it on Saturday."

Marge looked interested. "So you're getting involved in radio broadcasting?"

"Yes." I smiled. "I just started three months ago. It's fun!"

"You're a DJ!" Iris said. She clapped her hands and laughed.

"Well!" Nan sipped her wine. "You *have* been a busy girl!"

"And what new projects have you been doing, Nan?" I wanted to turn the conversation away from me. Nan always had some elaborate craft underway at her place.

She spoke eagerly, telling of her latest endeavor. I smiled and listened, watching her brown eyes sparkle with excitement. The thoughts in my heart were not for sharing. I enjoyed this time with my friends. They were dear to me. But my heart ached as I listened to them. How much longer could these friendships last?

(July)

David was overdue to receive his officer's evaluation report, the yearly assessment by his commanding officers. The OER would determine his future in the military. Since he had only one year left, he wasn't worried about it. In fact, he was so preoccupied, he hadn't thought about it at all.

The week after General Neil's intervention, Colonel Barnett handed David his OER. That night, David handed it to me.

"You need to read this, Lissa." He sank into the couch cushions and sighed.

I joined him on the couch and carefully read the report. I was used to seeing high performance credits on David's OER. But the praise from both Colonel Aiken and Colonel Barnett was profuse, totally unlike the demeaning lines they had been hammering into David the past few weeks:

Major McCloud administrates the Department of Radiology and Nuclear Medicine, supervising radiologists and nuclear medicine physicians as well as technicians and clerical personnel. He directs the performance of and interprets radiology examinations including bone, chest and abdomen, oral, intravenous and bladder contrast studies, ultrasound, mammography and computed tomography. He interprets MRI scans performed for Owen Army Hospital at civilian imaging centers. He oversees the Quality Improvement program. He consults with referring physicians and assures appropriateness of studies and good patient and physician relationships.

He possesses great depth and breadth of knowledge, skillfully applying this to clinical situations. He has superb judgment and clearly communicates with peers and subordinates. He is a dedicated, responsible medical officer of the highest integrity ... He always exceeded requirements.

Major McCloud, as Chief of the Department of Radiology, has performed in a singularly outstanding fashion. His contributions to the improvement of radiologic consultative services here have been many, with the focus on quality, access, and patient satisfaction. Despite critical personnel shortages in a downsizing environment, Major McCloud has been able to achieve a turnaround time of 5 days on all routine radiologic support. He has developed a superb quality improvement program, which involves the local Filipino radiologic community. Despite a large patient population, waiting times for routine and interventional studies have decreased to less than two weeks. Patient satisfaction is at an all time high. In addition, during this period Major McCloud achieved Radiology Board certification. Promoted ahead of contemporaries.

Major McCloud truly performed all his duties in an excellent manner in his first post-residency assignment as the chief of a multicultural department in a third-world country. Dedicated and energetic, he revitalized the personnel and upgraded the services to provide superb radiology support to the community. His clinical skills and intellectual interests constantly demonstrate his potential for a distinguished academic career. I strongly recommend his next assignment be on the teaching staff of a major medical center where he will be an ideal role model for the residents. He is unquestionably a future chief of a large training program and a consultant in radiology to the Surgeon General.

Wow.

I had, of course, read each of David's OERs. They were full of praise for his skill. This OER was no different, though maybe it did show a higher degree of satisfaction with his work. But even I could see that this one didn't fit with what had been happening at work. How could a commander harass David for an hour or more, several times a day, two or three times a week, trying to coerce him into illegal activities, then write such an evaluation?

David fingered the OER. "I wonder if they're afraid of General Neil, and if they intend to use this flattery to get around my resistance, since intimidation has not worked."

His suspicion was right.

(August)

Only a week later, Colonel Aiken ordered David to allow the Smithsonian Institution to use the radiology equipment for examining core samples. Yet when David had first arrived in the Philippines, the commander had given him a written order to *not* let the Smithsonian use the equipment because the JAG had deemed it illegal.

Military hospitals exist solely for the use of military members and their dependents. They are run on very tight budgets. Just the week before, we had read in the *Stars & Stripes* that a colonel had been court-martialed for taking his mistress to Owen Army Hospital for treatment. The inspector general and the JAG took such infractions seriously.

David showed Colonel Aiken the written order from the previous year, signed by the colonel's own hand, and informed him he would need a written counter-order from both the colonel and the JAG in order to proceed.

General Neil had left on vacation. Feeling safe, Colonel Aiken blew up at David again. The pressure was back on. The harassment picked up where it had left off, with hours of taking David away from work, yelling at him, and humiliating him. The fraudulent time cards again became an issue.

Over the past few weeks, I had watched David grow weaker. He was easily exhausted on our evening walks. His hands were clammy all the time, unusual for him. He developed a fever. Then I noticed he looked pale. Something was wrong. Earlier lab tests showed his bilirubin was two-and-a-half times normal, indicating he was having a problem that involved his liver. But the cause had not yet been determined.

Was his illness some tropical virus he picked up on a medical mission trip? Did it indicate some other illness? Or could the high bilirubin mean there had indeed been some sorcerer's brew in that cup of coffee that preceded his tachycardia? We had no answers. I felt that David needed tests and treatment in the States, but he was toughing it out, not able to trust the doctors involved in the situation here.

"David, your face is yellow!" I exclaimed one day when David came home for a lunch date. The children were having a play date at a friend's house.

He shook his head. "I haven't been feeling well for some time, Lissa. My head hurts constantly. Nothing seems to alleviate the pain. I feel tired and weak."

"You need to see a doctor, one you can trust. There's something seriously wrong, honey."

That afternoon, David put in a request to be sent to Tripler Army Medical Center in Hawaii for tests.

The commander refused. Instead, he ordered him to see the staff psychiatrist, Colonel Kant.

6

OPEN THREAT

David's narrative:

I'm in way over my head. I called Brian Newall about the situation and told him about the order to see the staff psychiatrist.

He said, "That's illegal! We have a new law protecting service members from psychiatric retaliation.[2] He can't do this to you. Make your commander put the order to see the psychiatrist in writing. That will buy you some time."

I told Colonel Aiken that his order was illegal according to the new law protecting service members from psychiatric retaliation, and that he would have to put his order in writing before I would meet with the psychiatrist. That stopped him for a while. He fumed and ranted at me, but gave no written order.

Then I called General Lamar, the oversight general at Tripler, and asked for help. When he was here a few months ago, he said that if I ever needed anything, to just call him. But he wasn't in the office and he didn't return my call. I faxed him the information later that week, but never heard from him. He did, however, contact Colonel Aiken and tell him of my report, which made Colonel Aiken even angrier.

I don't know what to do. When I joined the army, I took an oath to protect the Constitution of the United States. I did not sign up to do the dirty work of this colonel!

Honor is important to me. I have a son. He looks to me to learn what a Christian man is supposed to be like. I need to model honor for him. I need to model faith. If I break the law and end up facing court-martial and maybe prison time, how can I teach my son honor? If I fail to trust God by taking what seems the easy way out and fail to do what is right, how can I teach my son faith? I will stand by my decision to keep out of this illegal activity. There's no avoiding the fact that it's going to cost me. But I'm leaving that in God's hands.

This afternoon, when my commanders were again harassing me, Colonel Aiken said, "If you don't get on board and start cooperating, your family will not be safe."

Immediately afterward, Dr. Dias, one of the Filipino surgeons, came to my department on the pretext of checking the results of a patient's tests. He told me, "The roads around here aren't safe. I know of a school bus that tipped over on the way to school a few years ago. It caught fire. All those children became crispy critters." Then he laughed and walked away. Coming so soon after Colonel Aiken's warning, it clearly sounded like a threat.

I never counted on endangering my family! Since the tachycardia incident, I have realized these are not empty threats. I went home for lunch and talked it over with Lissa.

THIS IS GETTING entirely out of hand." David ignored the lunch I'd put before him.

I couldn't eat, either. I felt like I was drowning, unable to escape the fear that swept over me. My children were in danger! This was unreal. Could this be happening in the United States Army? Who would threaten *children?*

"Lissa, I think I'd better call the Department of the Army inspector general at the Pentagon. Maybe he can help protect us."

My heart raced. It didn't take much foresight to see that David was in serious trouble.

Oh, God! My heart cried out. What will happen to our children's faith if they see their father destroyed for his? Will they turn their backs on you? Will they walk away from your truth because of suffering and disillusionment? What should we do?

In that moment, God spoke very clearly to my spirit. "Lissa, your children's faith is not your responsibility. It is not your business—it is mine. Your responsibility and David's is to do what is right. I will take care of your children."

It was as though God had thrown me a life preserver. Yes. I could trust God to guard my children's faith. I already trusted him for my own, and over the years he had kept me through pain and sorrow and hardship. He was completely trustworthy. I could accept this word from him.

"Okay, David. Do what you have to do. I'm with you."

"All right. I'll call the Pentagon."

David's narrative:

Today I called the Pentagon. I spoke with the Department of the Army inspector general and told him what was happening. I told him about the threat to my family. He listened, but made no comments.

I asked if I should tell my commander that I had called him. Did he think that might protect my family and me? He said it was entirely up to me. He couldn't advise me. He would look into my report.

That afternoon, I told Colonel Aiken and Colonel Barnett that I had reported the situation to the Department of the Army inspector general. They were furious, and I think they were a bit unnerved. I don't know if my report to the DAIG is enough to keep them at bay, to protect my family, but it's all I could think to do.

(Later that week.) Colonel Aiken and Colonel Barnett once again called me into the commander's office. The new deputy commander of administration was with them. He informed me that the commander had signed the altered time cards, and that I had no business objecting. He called me an upstart and told me I was way out of line. I tuned him out. I know that what's happening here is illegal.

When they were through yelling at me, I went back to work. My head was aching. I took a couple aspirin, but that didn't help. I am totally exhausted. I have a fever. When I look in the mirror, I can see my skin is slightly yellow. I don't know what's wrong with me.

(Three weeks later.) No word has come from the Department of the Army inspector general. Colonel Aiken finally gave me a written order to see the psychiatrist. I filed it for future legal reference and went to see Colonel Kant, as ordered.

He was an older man, familiar with the ways of the army. He said, "Dr. McCloud, I find nothing significantly wrong with you. But you need to understand that psychiatrists in the military are here to keep things running smoothly between the commanders and those serving under them."

I was taken aback. "Do you mean that if I don't go along with this colonel, I will face psychiatric retaliation?" This was a gross violation of medical ethics!

"I'm not going to say that!" He was angry; his face was flushed and his voice was raised. "I know you've been reporting things to the DAIG! Dr. McCloud, you need to understand that the military is involved in a lot of illegal things. The army is in countries Congress knows nothing about, doing things they're not authorized to do. That's just the way it is. Look, you took a medical scholarship from the army, now you'd better play ball. If you don't, I can see you falling on your sword within two weeks."

"I will not become involved in illegal activities!" I told him.

He sneered. "You think you're so much holier than the rest of us!"

"No, I'm just a small man, and I make mistakes. But I have a very big God, and I fear him more than I fear the army. I will not do this thing." With that, I walked out of his office.

In his report to the commander, Colonel Kant said I was functioning normally and that he found no fault with me.

This week, Colonel Aiken came to my department for a radiological procedure. He had developed a sudden illness and needed my help. I could see he seemed frightened. I asked if I could pray with him before I began, as I do with every patient. His look softened, and I prayed with him, then began the procedure.

It was a good moment. When he left, I felt that things would improve.

7

DIVIDED
(SEPTEMBER)

T HE CHILDREN RETURNED to school by the middle of August. It was now September. David and I had found a Christian school in the city, not far from our home. I felt the children needed to be with kids their own age. They caught the bus on the corner at seven each morning and returned at four each afternoon. They weren't thrilled with the school, but I thought they'd come to like it once they made some friends.

I'd been enjoying my work with the Christian radio station, putting together a weekly musical broadcast for the English-speaking community. I'd been brushing up on my Spanish. I even wrote a couple songs in that language for when we hoped to visit Ecuador to explore my working with the radio broadcasting team there. God had given me an unexpected gift in songwriting a few years earlier, and it was proving to be a delight, as well as a way to reach children for Jesus. Having my own two children back in school gave me the extra time to concentrate on my work.

The station manager, Max Flynn, and his wife, Linda, were about the same age as David and I. We had done a few things together, and Max had encouraged David through this difficult time. Max had contacts with a Christian radio station in Ecuador and had offered to help me find a position there when we finished in the Philippines. We all felt that if David could just get through this situation, he could finish his time with the military, and we could move on to Quito.

Then David became ill again. He was feverish and his hands were clammy. He couldn't stand for any length of time, and he complained of a bad headache. Worried about the situation at work and knowing his commander was looking for any weakness to use against him, he tried to go to work anyway. But by noon, he was home again.

I drove him to the emergency room, but David didn't trust the Filipino doctor who had treated him badly the last time. He wouldn't let the doctor draw blood. The doctor shrugged and gave him some pills to make him sleep.

After more than a week, David showed no signs of recovering. He was still feverish, restless, and had a severe headache. I called Colonel Aiken and asked that David be sent to Tripler Army Medical Center to find out what was wrong.

The commander jumped at the chance, but not in the way I expected …

David's narrative:

> Colonel Aiken ordered me to go to Tripler Army Medical Center for psychiatric evaluation. I am to leave tomorrow.
>
> Why is this happening to me? Why couldn't the command just leave me alone and let me treat patients? I'm no fighter! But I cannot and will not become involved in illegal activities. If I suffer for it, so be it. I just don't want to drag Lissa and the children into this.
>
> Father God, protect me from my enemies! Protect Lissa! Protect my children! "O my God, in You I trust! Do not let me be ashamed; Do not let my enemies exult over me!"[3]

Colonel Aiken's treachery blew me away. He was a physician! Couldn't he see that David's illness was physical? I was sure that he could. Devastated, I didn't know where to turn.

Once he was in Hawaii, David called and told me how to reach him at officers' quarters. The next day, he saw the staff psychiatrist. Again, the psychiatrist found nothing wrong. David told him of the situation at Owen Army Hospital, and the psychiatrist thought it would be good for him to take a stress management class.

That week, Colonel Aiken disappeared from the hospital. Rumors were rampant that General Neil, who was now back from vacation, had relieved him of command. Nobody knew why, but many speculated that Colonel Aiken was involved in illegal activities. Colonel Barnett was now the acting commander.

David called me every day from Hawaii. He was feeling much better; his fever and headaches had disappeared. He looked forward to returning home. He had also communicated with his congressman in California, who had requested copies of the time cards. David had me send them. Congressmen have the authority to tell the military to stop harassing service members and even to release them, if the situation warrants it. David was hoping for an intervention.

Then the second blow fell. The psychiatrist at Tripler, Colonel Monroe, called Colonel Barnett and said, "There's nothing wrong with Dr. McCloud. I'm sending him back."

But Colonel Barnett told him, "I will not have him back until he has spent at least four days on a psychiatric ward."

Tripler Army Medical Center's chief of psychiatry didn't want to have anything to do with this. But someone at Tripler authorized the retaliation to continue. At Colonel Barnett's request, Colonel Monroe called other army medical centers to see if anyone would take David. The others wouldn't touch this case, either. For three weeks he tried, without success.

Finally he found a place in Oklahoma: Spires Army Medical Center. The deputy commander of clinical services, Colonel Austin, was a friend of Colonel Aiken. He agreed to take David.

Back in the Philippines, I was frantic. I tried to hide the problem from the children. Yet I could see that Ryan had some understanding of the situation. He just looked at me solemnly when I told them that Dad would be in the hospital for a while and wouldn't be coming home that week. Suzanna accepted it, but wanted to know if her daddy was very sick.

I shook my head and told her I didn't think he was, but that the doctors wanted to check him.

My anger doesn't lie close to the surface. It takes a long time and a lot of pushing before I become angry. But once I reach that point, the anger stays with me. Now flames of fury seemed to burn in my heart. I felt betrayed.

We're Americans! David has rights, doesn't he? What about that new law Brian mentioned—the law to protect military members from psychiatric retaliation? Why weren't those doctors obeying it?

I didn't know what to do, but prayer was at the top of my list. It was the first time in my life that the Psalms came alive to me. It was a comfort to see that King David faced times of frustration and anger, too—and that God accepted the angry prayers along with the others, preserving them through the centuries for others, like me.

Arise, Lord! Lift up your hand, O God. Do not forget the helpless. Why does the wicked man revile God? Why does he say to himself, "He won't call me to account" … Break the arm of the wicked and evil man; call him to account for his wickedness …[4]

On the wicked he will rain fiery coals and burning sulfur; a scorching wind will be their lot. For the Lord is righteous, he loves justice; upright men will see his face.[5]

I prayed those verses, and many others, back to God, following in the psalmist's steps.

My faith in God was in crisis. How could God let this happen to my David, the godliest man I knew? I had poured my heart out in prayer day after day, expecting God to rescue him. David had cried out to God for help. Yet he was being hounded without mercy.

Then the Lord reminded me of Hebrews 11, the great faith chapter of the Bible that tells of many who received miracles from God because of their faith. But the latter part of the chapter records a different story, that of those who stood up for God and were destroyed for their faith:

Others were tortured and refused to be released, so that they might gain a better resurrection. Some faced jeers and flogging, while still others were chained and put in prison. They were stoned; they were sawed in two; they were put to death by the sword. They went about in sheepskins and goatskins, destitute, persecuted and mistreated—the world was not worthy of them. They wandered in deserts and mountains, and in caves and holes in the ground. These were all commended for their faith, yet none of them received what had been promised. (Hebrews 11:35–39)

I felt confused and conflicted. God had been rescuing, preserving, and caring for me all my life. He had done the same with David. Yes, we had each gone through some difficult times that had seemed impossible. But *this!* This was so much more horrific! What good could come of it? How could God let this happen?

I called David's parents and told them what was happening. "Mom, pray for us! Have your friends pray for David!"

Lewis and Ruth McCloud were distraught over this turn of events. Lewis was furious. This was not the military he had supported all these years! What was wrong with America? Ruth was holding her emotions in, but her voice trembled, and I knew she was greatly distressed. I didn't know how to comfort them.

"Twentieth century history demonstrates that doctors have been recruited as agents of state sponsored torture, murder, and 'experimentation.' A physician who participates in such acts of his own free will, in direct violation of his duty to preserve life and decrease suffering, deserves to be treated as a criminal. What is a worse crime than harnessing the advances in knowledge and science for an evil purpose? All medical interventions should be undertaken with express informed consent and to help and never harm the patient."

Charles S. Yanofsky, M.D.[6]

8

TRAPPED
(OCTOBER)

David's narrative:

I am in way over my head. Before I flew to Oklahoma, I went to see the JAG and had a power of attorney made for Lissa. I had it sent to her via certified mail. She may need it. I don't know what the future holds for me.

The psychiatrist at Tripler, Colonel Monroe, sent me to Spires Army Medical Center in Oklahoma. When I arrived, I told the psychiatrist who met me that I was not willing to be admitted to the psych ward; if she did put me there, it would be considered an involuntary admission. I told her I was sent there in retaliation for reporting illegal activities against my commander, and that military law forbade this action. I reminded her that neither Colonel Kant nor Dr. Monroe had found anything abnormal about my thinking, that I was being admitted without diagnosis.

The Spires Chief of Psychiatry, Colonel Black, is a tall, red-headed woman with cold eyes. She said, "Major McCloud, nobody is as perfect as you represent yourself to be. We are going to keep you here and find out if you really are who you say you are."

Fear shot through me. I feel trapped. But Colonel Monroe, back in Hawaii, has assured me this would just be a four-day admission. I can stay calm for four days. Brian suggested I not talk to the psychiatrists at all, if possible. I'll try that.

I called Lissa and told her what was going on.

TRAPPED

MIZ LISSA, YOU must eat!" Marina reached across the corner of the table and placed her hand on my arm.

Our children were at the table eating breakfast. Suzanna was sharing her sausages with little Rosy, Marina's daughter, one piece at a time. Rosy was laughing, her big brown eyes fixed on Suzanna's face. Ryan glanced at me from time to time, his face solemn, listening for any bit of information about his dad.

I looked up from my plate and met Marina's compassionate eyes. It had been four weeks since David had flown to Hawaii, then to Oklahoma. While he was away, I could barely force myself to eat. I could barely sleep. Early every morning before the children awoke, I walked around the fort, following the paths David and I had walked together, choking back tears, wondering what to do. Then I came back and sat with the children during breakfast, not able to eat a thing. After they were in bed at night, I walked around the fort again in the dark.

I discovered that the McDonald's on fort was open round the clock, and I found I could swallow their chocolate milkshakes. That was all I had been able to get down for four weeks: two milkshakes a day.

I smiled at Marina. "I'll be okay."

The children were finished eating.

"Brush your teeth," I reminded them.

They raced off to get ready for the school bus, and dashed out the door.

Marina cleared the table, and I went upstairs to make the beds. Catching a glimpse in the mirror, I saw my clothes were a bit loose. I dug through a box in the closet and found a blouse and slacks in a smaller size. As long as I had something that fit reasonably, that was good enough.

My heart was in Oklahoma with David. What could I do to help him? Part of a Bible verse came to mind: "Men loved darkness instead of light because their deeds were evil."[7]

I sat in the oversized chair next to the bed. So far, everything that had happened to David had been done in private. What would happen if I shined some light on this great evil and started telling people? Word would fly like wildfire. Maybe the news would reach people in authority who would help. I didn't even know who that might be. But God did.

I sighed and reached for the telephone. Better get started.

David's narrative:

(Week 1) I feel like I'm in prison. First, they took everything away from me … except my Bible. They made me wear a blue outfit that identifies me as a psychiatric patient. I've been assigned to a resident psychiatrist—a guy just one year out of medical school. He does not have much experience at diagnosis and treatment.

He asked me a lot of questions, but I kept quiet and stonewalled him. He wrote on my chart that I'm "autistic." I can't believe this. But I just have to keep quiet for three more days, and they'll send me back to work …

… The patients on the ward are unpleasant. One of them, a very large man, becomes violent with no provocation and has to be restrained. He is dangerous.

… Racial tensions are running high on this ward, not only between patients, but also between staff and patients. I've seen significant violence. It's safer in my room than in the halls or lounge.

Another patient, an ordinary looking man, came up to me and, with an evil grin, said, "I know why you're here, Major!" A string of obscene accusations poured from his lips, taunting me. When I walked away, he shouted more obscenities after me.

There's a woman patient who sits in the lounge, curled up in a ball, and cries all day …

… My head aches constantly. I feel better when I lie down. I don't like going out of my room because of the constant conflict among patients and the loud noises. My only solace is my Bible. I find the Psalms particularly comforting. The psychiatrist seems to be offended that I spend so much time reading it, but I don't care. I just tune him and everyone else out. I don't know any other way to survive this ordeal …

… I haven't been allowed to eat for twenty-four hours now. I've asked, but the nurses tell me I have to be escorted to the dining room, and there's nobody to take me …

… The psychiatrist asked me a lot of filthy, humiliating questions today. Questions that implied he thought I was highly immoral. When I didn't answer, he told me they are going to keep me here for observation for a couple weeks.

What happened to release in four days?

My only link with hope is Lissa. I call her every day, and it helps to hear her voice. She's in my corner.

(Week 2) The psychiatrist asked me today about my religious beliefs. I told him, "I believe that all people are sinners. Not one of us is good enough to go to heaven, but God loved us so much that he sent his only Son, Jesus, into this world to die for our sins. He was crucified on a cross, buried, and rose again the third day, and is now with God the Father in Heaven. Everyone who believes in Jesus, who trusts in him, is saved from the penalty of sin and will one day be permitted into heaven. Jesus promised that someday he would return to earth to rule and reign. Before he returns, there will be a time of great tribulation. Christians who are living on earth at that time will be caught up into the air to be with Jesus. We call this 'the rapture.'"

The psychiatrist told me I am hyper-religious and delusional because of my beliefs, and he wrote that on my chart. If he diagnoses me as delusional, I will be put on the National Practitioner Data Bank of unfit physicians and will no longer be able to practice medicine! My life's work would be down the drain. Forever.

He has changed my diagnosis several times. First it was autism, then it was schizophrenia, then it was psychosis, then it was delusional … then it was major depression.

That would be like my saying a patient sent to radiology had "appendicitis … no, its pancreatitis … no, it's heart blockage … no, wait … it's brain cancer!" I'd get thrown out of the field of medicine for that. These psychiatrists don't know what they're doing. They're just guessing.

… The psychiatrist told me he wants to prescribe electric shock to treat my "delusions"! That amounts to torture. I told him no. He said he's going to do it anyway …

… The psychiatrist keeps asking me if I am suicidal. I have repeatedly told him no. He wrote in my chart that I am suicidal. They have moved my room to a place just across the hall from the six elevators for the hospital. The elevator closest to my room is an open shaft to the ground floor. There is only a yellow ribbon across the opening that says "men at work." I am afraid …

Back in the Philippines, I was terrified for David. He told me the psychiatrist said he's going to treat David with electric shock! When he told me the doctor had written "suicidal" on his chart, I said, "Honey, I'm taking the next plane out. I'll be there as soon as possible. Hold on, David!"

I hung up and called the resident who was serving as his doctor. My heart pounded. How could I stop that man from hurting David? Reserves of strength rose to the surface as the phone rang. I could do this. I *had* to!

"Dr. Carver speaking."

"This is Lissa McCloud. I am calling because my husband told me you want to use electric shock on him."

"Yes, Mrs. McCloud. I think it will help him. He's delusional."

"He is *not!* He has a fever that comes and goes, and he's physically ill. He's been having severe headaches. He needs to be seen by an internal medicine doctor or a tropical diseases specialist!"

"That isn't what we think here at Spires." He sounded patronizing.

"Listen to me: Don't you dare use electric shock on him, or I'll sue your socks off!"

"Lady, I can do anything I want to your husband, and you can't touch me! I'm a *military* doctor!"

"Don't you think I won't get you!" I said. "*You* are acting in violation of *military law!* So don't you *touch* David!"

I slammed the phone down and sat staring at the wall, trembling with fury, praying for God to spare my husband.

My next call was to Brian Newall, David's JAG friend. "Brian, the hospital commander has had David involuntarily admitted to the psychiatric ward at Spires, and they won't let him go."

"Lissa, this is highly illegal! I'm faxing you a copy of the new directive about this. It should help. Turn on your fax machine."

"Thank you, Brian."

"Let me know how this turns out."

I hung up and waited for the fax. As soon as it arrived, I called the airline counter at the Manila airport. I didn't dare go through a military ticket agent, for word would get out that I was flying to the States ... alone.

"There is a flight from Manila to Narita, Japan, that leaves tomorrow morning at six, arriving in Narita at approximately noon ..." The man at the ticket counter at Manila airport detailed the flight plan while I scribbled the information on a scratch pad. "Would you like me to book that for you, ma'am?"

"Yes, please," I said, then gave him my billing information.

I couldn't take the children with me. The flight itself would be brutal, and when I arrived in Oklahoma, who knew what I would find? I couldn't leave them alone in a motel while I fought to free their father. I could not take them with me to the hospital, either. I would have to speak with many people, and it would traumatize the children to hear what would be said. It was better that they stayed in the Philippines. But for their safety, no one could know I was gone.

I signed a permission slip for Marina to care for the children, stating she could sign for any medical treatment they might need in my absence.

"Marina, tell no one that I am gone," I said. "These wicked people must not know that the children are here alone!"

"I will keep them safe, Miz Lissa."

When the children arrived home from school, I told them Daddy needed me to help him and that I would have to fly to Oklahoma for a week. Ryan took it solemnly. But Suzanna cried, "Mommy! Don't leave me!"

It wrung my heart. I held her close and promised I would be back in a week. "Marina will be with you. She will keep you safe. She loves you! I have to go help Daddy, honey. I'll be back!"

But Suzanna wouldn't be comforted. The next morning, I had to leave before they went to school. Suzanna sobbed as I walked out the door. "Mommy! Don't leave me! Don't leave me!"

I wrapped my arms around her. "I'll be back soon, honey. Don't cry!" Tears poured down my cheeks. How could I leave my children in this country while I flew back to the States? How could I leave my darling Suzanna, who was terrified of being left behind?

The hardest thing I have ever done in my life, before or since, was to leave my children in the Philippines while I flew halfway around the world to try to save David, whose life was in danger. The entire time I was away, I feared for my children. But I had to place them into God's hands for safekeeping. I had no other choice.

9

RESCUE ATTEMPT
(MID-OCTOBER)

MY ROUTE TO David took me to Narita, Japan, where I took a flight to Honolulu, then to Los Angeles and Tulsa, Oklahoma. Then I faced a three-hour drive to Spires Army Medical Center.

I tried to sleep on the plane. But my fears for David's safety preyed on my mind, and my sleep was troubled. It took me over twenty hours of airtime, plus several hours waiting for connecting flights, then the long drive to Fort Hardin before I could rest. It was just past one in the morning when I checked into a motel outside the fort. It was cold in Oklahoma, and I shivered as I walked to my room. Too tired even to undress, I tossed my small suitcase and purse onto a chair, fell into bed, and pulled the covers over my head.

The wake-up call came at six. Dragging myself out of bed, I hit the shower. It felt good to get the smell of airports and airplanes out of my hair. Standing in front of the mirror wearing a light robe, my hair lying damp on my shoulders, I reached for the makeup. The dark circles under my eyes testified to my many sleepless nights.

I hadn't seen David in six weeks. Fear and anxiety had taken their toll. The clothes I had worn on the plane were too loose, so I'd picked up a few things in Honolulu during my brief layover. Size 4. Just six weeks earlier, I'd been a size 10 and wishing there were fewer inches around my waist. Now my ribs showed and my cheeks were hollow.

I dressed in navy slacks and a peasant blouse and sprayed a light touch of White Shoulders at my throat. It was David's favorite scent. Donning a poncho, I hurried out for a quick breakfast. There was no way I could face the ordeal that lay ahead without some food. And one look in the mirror had shown there was no question: I needed to eat!

At eight o'clock I pulled into Fort Hardin. The guard directed me toward the hospital. Red and gold leaves blew through the air on a stiff breeze. An overcast sky held back the sun. There on a hill, like a great hulking beast, stood Spires Army Medical Center, gray against the lowering sky.

I stopped the car and leaned my head on the steering wheel. "Oh, God! Help me know what to do and say! I can face this enemy only in your strength. Help me to free David!"

I took a deep breath and walked toward the hospital entryway. Its white columns standing against the gray bricks resembled giant saber teeth guarding a huge mouth. I moved toward the glass doors and entered the maw of the beast. Somewhere deep in its belly, my husband awaited.

To the left, I noticed a sign that read, "Inspector General." Yes. After I saw David, I would return here. But where was David?

I looked at the huge directory on the wall. What? The psychiatric ward was on the thirteenth floor! I shook my head. This hospital was clearly playing manipulative games with its patients, preying on the superstitious beliefs of so many. The thirteenth-floor designation for broken and fragile people was a portent of those doctors' malevolence. A chill ran down my back.

Taking the elevator, I swiftly rose to the thirteenth floor. The door opened and I looked around. There were six elevators, three on each side of the open area. I stepped into the hallway. Yes, there was a nurses' station. I walked toward it, glancing at the patients' rooms. I didn't see my husband.

Two nurses sat behind the counter. They were both very large women. One stepped up to the counter. "May I help you?"

"Yes. I am Mrs. McCloud. I'm here to see my husband, Dr. David McCloud."

"Oh," she said, her eyes opening wide.

The second nurse stopped her charting and looked up.

"Why is your husband here?" the first nurse asked in a low voice. "There isn't anything wrong with him!"

"He's here because his commander is involved in illegal activities, and David reported it. His commander is doing this to discredit David's testimony."

Her eyes opened wider, then she swore. "When my stint is up, I'm gettin' outta here!" She pointed down the hallway where I'd just come. "Your husband is down there—room 112."

I walked quickly down the hall. There it was. The door was closed. I knocked. "David?"

The door opened, and I flew into his arms. "Oh, David! Oh, David!"

He held me close a long while. "Lissa! You're here!"

I could feel how thin he was. And I could sense his humiliation at having to wear the blue hospital garb worn only by mental patients. His body was warm and damp. He still had that mysterious fever. But we were together now, and surely God would help me tear him out of the hands of these sadists.

We sat together on the edge of the bed, David's arm around my shoulders.

"When are you coming home?" I asked.

"I don't know. First they said four days. Then they changed it to an additional week. Now they're saying two more weeks."

Feeling his ribs, I remembered the nurses often kept him from eating. "Have you eaten anything today?"

"No. They said there's no escort ... again."

"Let's go to the nurses' desk and ask." I arose, holding onto his hand and tugging.

As we exited the door, I noticed an open elevator shaft across from his room. I walked over and looked down. It was a long, long way to the ground ... and David said the resident had labeled him suicidal. My heart began to pound. I had to get him out of here! I knew he wasn't suicidal—I'd been talking to him every day on the phone. But this looked very dangerous ... and I had learned not to trust the military psychiatrists.

At the desk, I asked the nurse to whom I'd just spoken, "May I please take my husband down to the dining room?"

She hesitated and looked at the chart, her eyes troubled. "Yes. But you need to have him back here in an hour. That's when the doctors come back. He's not supposed to leave the ward today."

"Thank you." I slipped my arm into David's and headed for the elevators. We stepped inside and the door slid closed.

"The dining room is on the ground floor." David punched the button.

When the door opened, we stepped out toward the dining room. I stopped. The door right next to it was the morgue. The dining room and the morgue shared a wall, and the doors were not twenty feet apart. Who had designed this building!

"Come on." David eyed the dining room.

"Okay," I said. David probably didn't even notice the odd set-up. He was a doctor. Medical people think differently than others. I remembered his first semester of medical school when he brought home a human skeleton to study. We were using our large closet for his books and desk, so David wanted to keep the skeleton in the only place not yet in use: under our bed!

I strongly opposed that, but he eventually convinced me to do it his way. I let him store our bony guest under our bed—but on David's side, not mine!

Remembering the oddities of doctors didn't help with how I felt about the morgue and kitchen sharing the same wall. It grossed me out, and I was indignant at the military designers. I couldn't even drink a cup of tea that first day, thinking of the close proximity of the dead. But David was famished, and he ate well.

Afterward, we found a quiet place in the hospital garden to talk. With his arms around me, David whispered, "I thought they would take you away from me, Lissa!"

"Never!" I said. "Nothing could ever keep me from you, David!"

He stroked my face and looked into my eyes. I leaned against him and wept. He comforted me. Just feeling his arms around me gave me hope.

Before we knew it, an hour had flown and David had to return to his imprisonment. When we stepped off the elevator we were met by a very angry young man wearing the white jacket of a doctor.

"Where have you been, Mr. McCloud?"

I looked at the captain's bars on his uniform. The voice was familiar. This must be the resident who was playing with David's life. Yes, his name tag said "Carver." I lifted my chin. "It's *Doctor* McCloud!"

"He is not to leave this ward without my express permission!"

"Since you're here now," I said, "let's go into your office, *Captain* Carver." I turned and smiled at David. "I'll talk to you in a little while, honey." Turning back toward the resident, my smile faded.

He marched down the hall and I followed him into his office.

He shut the door firmly. "Mrs. McCloud."

"Captain Carver, my husband is feverish. He does not belong on this ward."

"Your husband is mentally ill."

"No, he is not." I faced him squarely and looked him in the eyes. "He was found mentally fit by *two* army psychiatrists! He is here because his commanding officers are involved in illegal activities, and he reported them. They have had him committed involuntarily—with no diagnosis—to this ward to discredit him before the Department of the Army inspector general's investigation."

"It doesn't matter what his commanding officers are doing." He shook his head. "He is mentally ill, and we're going to treat him for that. His commanding officers said he was too tired to work and seemed stressed. We've examined him and find him to be delusional. We're going to treat him for that."

"You'd better not," I said. "In case you weren't aware, there is a new law prohibiting psychiatric retaliation against service members who report illegal activities."

"That doesn't matter. It doesn't apply here. What matters is that *I* say your husband is mentally ill."

I tried hard to stay calm. "He has a fever. His bilirubin is two-and-a-half times normal. He has blinding headaches. This is a *physical* illness, not mental!"

"You are not a doctor," he said. "This is *mental* illness!"

Anger and frustration like I had never known welled up within me. "You *idiot!*" I hurled the words at him. *"Can't you see that his skin is yellow?"*

It was not one of my stellar moments. Never had I spoken to anyone in that manner. I could see that nobody had ever spoken to Captain Carver like that, either. He didn't know where to look, and his face was red and he looked like he was about to explode.

Yet I couldn't feel guilty about my words—not with the threat hanging over David's life. Not with "suicidal" written on his chart and his room next to an open elevator shaft. This man was not just ignorant, he was evil.

I stood. "I am in contact with David's congressman, the Department of the Army inspector general, and the JAG. I want my husband released."

"No."

"You will be hearing more from me." I turned and left the room.

It was time to go over this man's head.

I walked back to David's room and wrapped my arms around him. I told him what had just happened. "Honey, I am going to talk to the hospital IG and try to see the hospital commander about this. I'll be back as soon as I can."

He kissed me, hope flickering in his eyes, and released me to my errand.

10

DEATH OF OUR DREAMS

ATCHING A GLIMPSE of myself in the mirror, I saw the red flags flying in my cheeks. My fury showed. I needed to calm down. Taking a deep breath, I walked toward the elevators, rode down to the entry level, and headed for the inspector general's office. His office was next to the lobby. I knocked on the door, and a pleasant male voice called, "Come on in."

I walked into the first room and saw an office with a smiling young man coming through the door.

"May I help you?"

"Yes. Are you the inspector general of the hospital?"

"Yes. I'm Major Duggan. Ben." He reached out his hand. "And you are?"

I took his hand. "I'm Lissa McCloud. Can I have a few minutes of your time?"

"Of course." He ushered me into his office. "Have a chair."

I sat and took a deep breath. I was not yet used to talking to people in military authority, and I quaked inside. But I tried to keep calm and businesslike.

"How can I help you, Mrs. McCloud?"

"My husband, Dr. David McCloud—a major—reported his commander for illegal activities. To discredit him, the commander had him involuntarily committed to the Spires Army Medical Center psychiatric ward. This is in violation of a recently passed law, the Mental Health Evaluation of Members of the Armed Forces Directive."

I laid my copy of the directive on Major Duggan's desk. He began scanning it. Returning to the date at the top of the directive, he said, "It was issued last year."

"If you will look at page two." I leaned forward and pointed to the section:

3. No person shall refer a member for a mental health evaluation as a reprisal for making or preparing a lawful communication to a Member of Congress, any appropriate authority in the chain of command of the member, an inspector general (IG) or a member of a DoD audit, inspection, investigation, or law enforcement organization.

4. No person shall restrict a member from lawfully communicating with an IG, attorney, Member of Congress, or others about the member's referral for mental health evaluation.

5. Any violation of subsections D3 or D4, above, by any persons subject to the UCMJ (Uniform Code of Military Justice) is punishable in accordance with the provisions of paragraph 34a.

I flipped the page and pointed to the next section.

The Secretaries of the Military Departments shall a) Within 120 days of the date of this Directive, publish an implementing regulation that provides that violations of the prohibitions referenced in subsections D3 or D4, above, by persons subject to the UCMJ are punishable as a violation of Article 92 of the UCMJ.

Ben looked up. "So. This law is currently in effect."

"Yes, it is." I looked him in the eye. "I'm here to try to get my husband out."

Major Duggan's face went blank. "Um, Mrs. McCloud, I'll have to look into this. May I make a copy of this?"

"Please do."

"Major Duggan," I said, "two army psychiatrists examined him and gave him a clean bill of health. But his commanding officer insisted that David be incarcerated for four days in a psychiatric ward before allowing him back to work. It has now been almost three weeks. I will try to speak with the hospital commander next, and I have to drive back to Tulsa tomorrow evening to catch an early morning flight back to the Philippines. Can you help me?"

"I will try, Mrs. McCloud." He looked concerned. Returning from the photocopier a few minutes later, he handed me my original copy of the directive.

"Thank you, Major Duggan." I stood to leave. "By the way, this case is under investigation by the Department of the Army inspector general."

He froze for a moment. Then he walked me to the door. "Come to my office tomorrow after lunch and I'll have some answers for you."

"Okay." I nodded. "Which way to the commander's office?"

"General Martin's office is that way." He pointed me in the right direction. "Good luck, Mrs. McCloud."

"Thanks."

At least he was positive and friendly.

As the office door closed behind me, I walked toward the lobby and sank into a chair. I needed time to regroup for the next interview. "Lord Jesus," I prayed silently, "help me! Help me!"

A few minutes later, I headed down the hallway toward the commanding general's office. I saw a uniformed young woman through the opened door, talking on the phone. I walked in and waited.

"Yes?" She put her hand over the receiver.

"I would like to see General Martin."

"Just a moment." She concluded the call and walked to the counter where I waited. She was a very beautiful woman, the kind that always made me feel like a country girl in the city. "What would you like to discuss with the general?"

I repeated the summary to her.

Her eyebrows rose halfway to her hairline. "I'm sorry, but you'll have to speak with Colonel Austin, the deputy commander of clinical services. He handles these types of matters." She drilled me with steely eyes.

"Where is his office?"

"It's just down the hall. That way." She pointed, then turned her back on me and walked away.

I sighed and headed toward Colonel Austin's office. His door was closed. I knocked, and another secretary opened the door. She, too, was young and beautiful.

"May I help you?"

"I'd like to speak with Colonel Austin."

"I'm sorry. Colonel Austin's schedule is full."

"I am here on a brief trip from the Philippines, and I *must* speak with him."

"Let me check his schedule." She walked toward her desk and reached for an appointment book. "Okay. I can fit you in around ten o'clock tomorrow morning. What is your name?"

"Lissa McCloud."

"What may I tell him you wish to discuss?"

I told her. She paused, looking at me out of the corner of her eye. "Oooooo-kay." She made a scribble on the calendar.

"Thank you." I turned and left. I'd done all I could for the day. Now I needed to get back to David.

Back on the thirteenth floor, I arranged to take David to lunch. The nurse looked uncomfortable, but she allowed it—as long as I promised to bring him right back. He was supposed to be confined to the ward.

David and I ate together and spent the rest of the afternoon talking in his room and in the patient lounge. Then I took him downstairs to dinner. I knew the only way he would be allowed to eat was if I accompanied him. It infuriated me. I felt helpless because I knew that when I left, there would again be days when David would not be permitted to eat.

I stayed with him as long as the staff allowed. Back at the motel, I fell into a deep sleep, exhausted by the day's conflicts.

The next morning, after I had accompanied David to breakfast, I went to see Colonel Austin. He was a handsome, arrogant man, full of his own importance. When I told him what was happening, he laughed gently, as though to humor me.

"Mrs. McCloud," he said, "let's let the professionals decide what to do here. If you get three psychiatrists in a room, they can never agree on a diagnosis. If there's nothing to find, they will let me know. I trust my staff. You should, too."

"It is illegal," I said, "to put a service member in the psychiatric ward after he has reported illegal activities."

"Well, Mrs. McCloud, that is a matter for speculation. And I know Colonel Aiken. Are you accusing me of being in collusion with Colonel Aiken?"

"I have no idea," I said. "I *do* know that you are breaking the law, and I want you to release my husband immediately!"

"No. He will stay here until we are satisfied."

I walked out of his office in fury and headed for the elevators back to the thirteenth floor. There were pay phones on the way. Taking out my calling card, I put a call through to David's parents.

"Mom," I said, "I need you and Dad to come out here as soon as possible. They have labeled David suicidal and have placed his room next to an open elevator shaft that drops thirteen floors. His life is in danger. I don't think I'm going to be able to free him. You need to be here after I leave for the Philippines. I don't think they'll try anything with you here to watch over him, and I don't think they'll deny him food if you're here. He's just skin and bones as it is. I think you should be here to ensure he is allowed to eat and to see that they don't try anything. I'll try to get back soon. Maybe two weeks."

Ruth gasped. "We'll be on the next plane. Is there anything else?"

"Yes. I'll need Dad to try to find a JAG officer here at Fort Hardin to help get David out of this."

"Okay. And Lissa? We're praying for you both!"

"Thanks, Mom. I'll talk to you later tonight."

I placed the receiver back and tried to pull myself together. My hands were trembling. The confrontation with Colonel Austin had drained me. I wasn't used to speaking forcefully to officers ... or anyone else. But I could see this was a battle for David's life. It was going to take every ounce of strength within me to win. Did I have what it would take?

Heading back up to David's room, I felt empty and hopeless. I'd talked to everyone who might be willing to help, but no one cared. I stepped off the elevator and went to the desk to see if they would let David spend a few minutes with me in the garden before I had to leave for Tulsa.

I heard a shout. Down the hall, one of the very large nurses pushed a patient into his room. As she shoved him inside, she raised her fist and slammed it on the back of his neck. The patient shuddered under the blow, and she grabbed the door and pulled it shut.

I froze. How could I leave David here, where patients were abused, where doctors lied about him, placed him in jeopardy, and tempted him to kill himself ... or where someone could push him to his death? Bile rose in my throat. With great difficulty, I pulled myself together and walked toward the nurses' desk.

"Lissa, these people are going to destroy me. I know it."

David and I sat together on the lawn, leaning against the stone wall in the garden, our arms around each other. I had cried until there were no more tears.

"These psychiatrists will never let me return to my work in the Philippines. The children aren't safe there ... you know about the threats ... so don't wait for me. Get them to safety. Bring them to Oklahoma. I want you to use the power-of-attorney that I sent you to get our things shipped here. I know they haven't issued orders yet, but arrange it anyway. Find a house near the fort—but whatever you do, don't live on post. You would be under military control, and we can't afford to trust them. But stay close to me. I need you!"

"Of course, David. But I have to try to get you out of here!"

"It's no good, honey."

"I *have* to *try!*"

"No. You can't get me out. You must let them do what they intend to do with me. Stay out of it. These people are without honor or conscience.

They're dangerous. One of us needs to survive this—for the children's sake. Let God be the one to free me, if there is to be any deliverance from this."

"Okay, David." I wept, leaning on his chest, holding him close.

I didn't have any more time. I had to leave soon, and the IG, Major Duggan, had told me to stop by his office before I left for the airport. "Darling. I'll be here for you … always!" I kissed him hard. Together, we walked back into the building. At the elevators, we held each other in a long embrace; I could not bear to let David return to that ward.

Finally, David released me and stepped back into the elevator.

"I'll be back as soon as I can!" The doors slid shut between us. With tears in my eyes, I headed for the IG's office.

"Mrs. McCloud, come in," Major Duggan said solemnly. He ushered me to a chair and sat behind his desk. "I spoke with Colonel Austin about the law regarding psychiatric retaliation. He said the law has not yet been implemented—and that they don't have to obey it." He looked grim.

I was stunned. David was right. These people intended to destroy him. The law had not restrained them, and they did not fear it. All our years of preparation for the mission field, all our dreams, all our hopes came crashing down around me.

"This is the death of our dreams!" I burst into tears. Covering my eyes with both hands, I sobbed for several minutes.

"Thank you for trying to help, Major Duggan." I took the tissue box he pressed into my hands. "I need to drive back to the airport in Tulsa now. My flight to the Philippines leaves at seven in the morning. Please do what you can to protect David while I'm gone!"

"I will take a personal interest in him," he said. "Mrs. McCloud, let us find a room for you on post for the night. You shouldn't be driving in this condition!"

I could see his concern.

"Thank you, Major Duggan, but I'll be all right. I promise to stop at a motel if I get too tired." I stood.

He was reluctant to let me leave. Handing me his business card, he walked to the hospital doors with me, ushering me outside. "If you need anything, just call. And the name's Ben."

"Thank you, Ben." I smiled through the tears and walked back to the car. It was going to be a very long drive, and each mile's separation from David would break my heart a little more.

11

THE ADMIRAL

BACK IN THE Philippines, word of David's treatment had blown across the entire military community, and things began to happen quickly.

One of the men in our church had a brother who was a bodyguard for Admiral Grady, commander-in-chief of Pacific Command, stationed in Hawaii. Admiral Grady was spending some time at Subic Bay Naval Station, directing the investigation of regional drug smuggling from the Pacific to the mainland United States and developing strategies to interrupt the flow.

The bodyguard, Gerald Smith, had been at our church a number of times, and we were acquainted. Informed by his brother about what was happening to David, he told the admiral about the situation and vouched for David's character. Within days of my return to the Philippines, I found myself summoned to headquarters at Subic Bay to speak with the leading inspector general serving under Admiral Grady, and two other members of the admiral's staff: the army surgeon general of the Philippines and the general's own lawyer, Mr. Hollis, a former Navy JAG.

I wasn't looking forward to that long drive to Subic Bay, but I arose the next morning before dawn and started out, driving north toward Clark Air Base, then turning southwest toward the naval base.

The conversation with Gerald brought a breath of new life to my spirit. Maybe Admiral Grady would step in and rescue David! Driving toward Subic Bay, I prayed fervently. "Lord, thank you for sending help! Please use these men to free my David from those awful psychiatrists!"

I had called ahead to Subic Bay and arranged to stay in the guest quarters overnight. I didn't like being away from the children, but the drive back to Fort Duran was impossible after dark, and Marina would be with the children. I would arrive home the next afternoon.

I told Marina of my plans.

"The children are happier when you are here," she said. "While you are gone to the States, Suzanna had a most difficult time going to sleep. I had to sit in her room and pray for her so she would sleep. But I think they will be okay if you are just gone one night."

"You are so dear to me, Marina," I said. She was truly my sister in Christ. I hugged her. "I don't know what I would do without you."

Marina's eyes brimmed with unshed tears. "You are dear to me, too, Miz Lissa. I don't like that you go back to the States. I will miss you a lot."

I brushed tears from my eyes. "I'll miss you, too, my dear sister."

As I drove north, I thanked God for Marina and prayed for my children's peace.

When I finally reached Subic Bay, I was hot and tired. I checked into the guest quarters, showered, and changed into fresh clothes. Then I called Gerald and told him I was ready.

Gerald met me at the parking area outside headquarters and escorted me inside. Large tropical greenery grew around the building, drooping over the shady path. Moss grew in the cracks of the ancient sidewalk. Gerald ushered me through the door and into Colonel Farr's office, then quietly left, closing the door behind him.

Colonel Farr, the inspector general, Philippines, ushered me to a seat. Tall, with dark hair and gray sideburns, he exuded authority.

"Good afternoon, Mrs. McCloud." His voice was calm and deep. "Thank you for coming. I know this is a stressful time for you."

I had been instructed to bring a written report on the situation. Taking the seat Colonel Farr indicated, I pulled out the large envelope containing the report and laid it on his desk.

"Is this the report?" He reached for the envelope.

"Yes. I've put everything I can remember in it."

He scanned the contents while I looked around his office, nervous but reassured. The room was painted cream, with the same dark wood furniture found in all the other military posts on the island. The office smelled faintly of damp, old wood. The window behind his desk was water-stained, with large tropical plants rubbing against its shaded surface.

Colonel Farr had few questions when he finished examining the papers. "This is a very believable report, Mrs. McCloud. Thank you for providing it." He stood. "I will see what I can do to help your husband."

Later, Gerald told me that Colonel Farr reported to Admiral Grady he believed David was facing a credible threat of retaliation for his report of illegal activities. The admiral was considering what to do.

At two o'clock that afternoon, I spoke with the attorney, whose office was in an adjacent building. A pale, plain man, he listened to my words and said as little as possible. I couldn't tell if he believed me.

From there, Gerald took me to meet with the army surgeon general, Philippines, Colonel Duffy. He also served at Subic Bay Headquarters, though he was with the Army Medical Corps. It was more convenient for him to work out of that location, for his responsibilities covered the entire Philippine region.

"Mrs. McCloud," Colonel Duffy said, "your husband is not the first doctor who has faced this type of action at the hands of Colonel Aiken! He is, in fact, the third doctor *this year* who has faced psychiatric retaliation because he wouldn't go along with something Colonel Aiken wanted. I am going to do everything I can to help you. Here is a list of names and phone numbers of people you should speak with." He handed me a paper covered with hand-written information.

"Dr. Olsen and Dr. Peters have been treated this way, too," Colonel Duffy said. "When you get back to Owen Army Hospital, talk with them. Colonel Aiken has created a terrible atmosphere at that hospital. Everyone is afraid of everyone else, and nobody knows who is on what side."

"You'll also need to talk to Lieutenant Colonel Ingermann," Colonel Duffy added. "He was the chief of resource management at Owen Army Hospital, and I transferred him to my command so he could report on illegal activities without facing retaliation. He's now in Washington, D.C., serving at the Pentagon. He knows all about the time card fraud and much, much more. He has a copy of an IG report that he may be willing to share. What David has discovered is only the tip of the iceberg."

"Thank you, Colonel Duffy. I appreciate your help."

"Oh—and you should talk with Colonel Stapleton. He knows all about what's happening to the doctors here. He was the psychiatrist at this hospital before Colonel Kant, and he sent those doctors for psychiatric treatment on orders from Colonel Barnett. You will want to call him as well. He's back in the States—North Carolina, I think." He reached for another paper. "Let me give you his name and number, too."

"Colonel Duffy, exactly what is going on here? Why is Colonel Aiken doing these things?"

The surgeon general snorted. "We are in a drawdown here. Our lease with the Philippines will expire soon, and we do not think it will be renewed. President Aquino wants us out. When we leave the Philippines, the hospital will continue, run by their own people. I have sources in the

Filipino government who have said that Colonel Aiken wants to retire here. He has given broad hints that he wants to be the administrator of the hospital when we leave. To that end, instead of referring the Filipinos to the appropriate charity for aid, he has been using funds intended for our troops and their families to finance his own charity work, to gain prestige among the Filipinos. He crushes anyone who gets in the way of his goal."

That would explain it. But what about Colonel Barnett? Now that Colonel Aiken was reportedly relieved of command, why was Colonel Barnett continuing to destroy David? Was he into the corruption so deep, he had to discredit David to save himself?

Colonel Duffy stood. "Thank you for coming in, Mrs. McCloud."

I stood to go.

"Mrs. McCloud, you keep in touch with me. I'll do everything I can to help." He handed me his business card.

"Thank you, sir." As I walked back down the deeply shaded pathway with Gerald, I breathed a sigh of relief. At least now I had some help.

But I was puzzled. If the command at Subic Bay knew all about Colonel Aiken's illegal activities, why had they not relieved him of command earlier? And why didn't someone in command step in to rescue David now?

"Those are all the people you need to meet, Mrs. McCloud," Gerald said. "If there's anything else, I'll contact you. I'll be praying for you and David. Don't worry! We have a very big God."

"Yes, we do."

"Now why don't you just relax and enjoy Subic Bay for the evening? That drive back to Manila shouldn't be taken at night."

"Yes. I've booked a room at guest quarters for the night."

"Excellent." Gerald nodded.

Exhausted emotionally, I walked toward my room, grateful for all of Gerald's help. But I was far too tired to explore the naval base. I had a light dinner at the officers' club and went straight to bed.

Back at Fort Duran the next afternoon, I made appointments with the other physicians Colonel Duffy had named. When I met Dr. Olsen the next morning, he was scandalized that I knew about his embarrassment. He didn't want to talk about it. But Dr. Peters was an entirely different story. His spirit had not been broken.

It was late in the afternoon, after surgery hours and rounds, when I parked outside Owen Army Hospital. Huge trees towered over above my head. A gentle breeze blew off the Bay of Manila, cooling my face and ruffling my hair. Entering through the hospital basement, I took the elevator to Dr. Peter's office on the surgical floor.

I found his office, the door open, and knocked on the door frame.

"Mrs. McCloud? Come in. Please have a seat."

"Thank you." I sat on the hardwood chair. Medical books were stacked on one corner of the desk, and the book he was reading was pushed back.

"So what can I do for you, Mrs. McCloud? I haven't seen Dave in awhile."

I told him what was being done to David.

"What! Dave, too?" He was shocked. "Dave is one of the best radiologists I've ever met! He's a man who has his act together better than anyone else I know. How can this be?"

"Colonel Duffy said you experienced similar treatment," I said, not sure how he would respond. "He said you might be able to help us."

"If I can help by telling you what happened to me, I will."

Dr. Peters leaned back in his chair and began to tell me of his experience. "I'm a surgeon, and a good one," he said. "After I operate, I always tell the patient what he or she can expect. If I haven't been able to correct the problem, I say so. But the commanders don't like that. They wanted me to tell the patients that everything was okay, whether or not it was. They said my honesty opened them up to legal problems. I disagreed and refused to do what they asked. So they sent me to a military hospital in the States and had me committed to the psychiatric ward." His face was bleak. "There I was diagnosed as 'obsessive-compulsive.'" He swore. "*Every* good doctor is obsessive-compulsive! That's the nature of the profession."

He tapped his desk with a pencil, looking off into the distance.

"I figure I'll finish my time here, then go into civilian practice. Out in the real world, they'll recognize this was just a bunch of military nonsense." He shook his head. "Tell Dave what I went through. And I want you to keep me informed about him."

"I will. Thank you for being so open." So David wasn't the only one to experience this kind of retaliation from Colonel Aiken and Colonel Barnett. This was standard procedure. It horrified me.

That evening when David called, I told him about Dr. Olsen and Dr. Peters, and what Colonel Duffy had said.

David was appalled. "What's being done to the doctors at Owen Army Hospital is criminal!" He was silent for a moment. "If I must go through this psychiatric retaliation to put a stop to it, then so be it."

The next afternoon, I dropped by Dr. Peter's office and told him what David had said.

Dr. Peters shook his head. "I've seen heroes in movies, but I have had few in real life. I've been disappointed to see that most people are out to save their own skin. I have not seen many heroes ... until now. To me, Dave is a hero." He paused and looked down. "I'm not a religious man, but I have always admired Christ." With great emotion, he said, "Dave walks like Jesus Christ."

He frowned. "When this is all over and you and Dave are free from the military, send me a note and let me know how you are doing. I think Dave will do well on the outside, no matter what the military does to him."

"I will if I can," I said. "And thank you for your help."

I breathed deeply and walked back to my car. Dr. Peters' words echoed in my heart: *Dave walks like Jesus Christ.*

12

TIME TO LEAVE

AVID'S PARENTS ARRIVED at Spires Army Medical Center the day after I left. Their presence in Oklahoma allowed me to concentrate on the many arrangements for our move back to the States. Yet my heart continually prayed for my husband.

I placed ads at Fort Duran to sell David's boat and my car. The truck could be shipped back to the States. Turning my thoughts toward our possessions, I knew we were each limited to two suitcases. Everything else would have to remain in the Philippines until the army shipped it. What should we take?

At times like these, one learns what is important. I let the children pick which toys or games they wanted to take, and fitted them around the clothes they would need in the States. Most of my clothes no longer fit, so I packed very few personal items. Financial records, family photos, and music books filled my suitcases, making them incredibly heavy.

There was no way we could know how long David would be trapped at Spires, so I prepared to teach the children's school lessons at home again. I would need a few books for that. The American military bookstore had a great supply of materials for home-schooling. I headed there for a quick perusal.

I soon found the books I needed. As I walked to the cash register, I saw Nan Barnett coming toward me from the side aisle. I couldn't avoid her. I froze inside, not knowing what to do.

"Lissa," she said sweetly, "I heard about David. I'm so sorry about what's happened to him!"

My heart beat furiously. I cared deeply about Nan! She was so sweet and kind. But anything I said would be used against David. I could not bring myself to tell her what her husband was doing. She was bound to him, just as I was bound to my husband. I could not undermine her marriage by denouncing her husband! I didn't want her children to be shamed by their father, either. It didn't matter that Colonel Barnett was hurting David. What mattered in that moment was Nan. But there was nothing I could say that wouldn't seriously damage her. The battle lines had been drawn, and she stood on the other side. I stood there, my eyes straight ahead.

The clerk announced my total.

Without looking at Nan, I paid him and walked out. It was the only time in my life I had shunned anyone. I didn't know what else to do.

Back in the car, tears burned my eyes. I was not cut out for this! I leaned my head on the steering wheel and took a deep breath. It was time to get back to work ... I had so little time. But it was hard to see the road with tears in my eyes.

That evening after dinner, while Marina and I cleared the table, a brisk knock sounded at the door. It was our neighbors, Mark and Julie.

"Come in," I said. The last time I had seen them was the afternoon I'd flown to help David. I'd told Mark what was going on and had asked for his help, since he had been an inspector general. "Do sit down."

"Lissa," Mark said, "I've looked into your story and I've written a letter you can use any way you like to help get David out." He handed me a white, unsealed envelope.

I opened it and read his report:

To whom it may concern:

I have been asked to relate what I know as the working environment or conditions at Owen Army Hospital during the period that Major David McCloud was assigned there. I resided across the street from the McClouds while they lived on Fort Duran, Philippines. I was asked by Mrs. McCloud for advice based on the fact that I had prior experience as an army inspector general. I was shocked at her story and frankly thought it must contain some exaggeration because it did not seem possible. I decided to contact some officers I knew personally, that I knew I could trust for straight and honest answers.

I contacted an officer who worked at the post Staff Judge Advocate (legal) office. His response was one of surprise that I knew about the situation because it was very hush-hush. He related that there were numerous allegations against the hospital commander for illegal and unethical conduct. He said he was shocked at some of the evidence and that such conduct could take place within the US Army. He said it was his belief that anyone responsible for such actions would be convicted of criminal activities. He said that because of professional confidence he could not relate specifics, and that he could not comment specifically on the events with Major McCloud. But based on the facts he had, he could not discount or dismiss Mrs. McCloud's story as untrue or exaggerated.

I also spoke to an officer friend who worked in the hospital. He related that there were numerous irregularities in the hospital but that people (particularly the military) were afraid to say anything for fear of retribution. He said it was known that the officers responsible for the 'irregularities' had spies and informers and that people were reluctant to even talk about things. He described it as a 'reign of fear and terror' and that careers had been destroyed. I asked this officer to make a statement like this one, describing the atmosphere in the hospital that he was familiar with. He declined, citing a continuing fear of retribution, particularly for voluntary statements. He said he would willingly provide information if he should be subpoenaed.

I know an investigation was conducted last summer by the commander of the hospital at Ft. Higgs. It found numerous problems, though I have been unable to obtain a copy of the inspection report. The hospital commander retired last month. It is alleged that because of friends in high places, he was allowed to retire in lieu of facing a court-martial.

I have no first-hand knowledge of the alleged activities or conditions at Owen Army Hospital. But men I trust relate that things illegal and unethical were conducted by senior personnel at the hospital. These individuals attempted to coerce others to participate or remain silent about their actions, or their careers would be ruined. They say the hospital was a stressful place to work with strong feelings of distrust and suspicion. I believe them.

Mark Ralston
Major, U.S. Army

Feeling courage seep back into my heart, I looked up and met Mark's eyes. His clear, blue eyes held mine.

"Mark, I can't begin to thank you!" While all the other military people were merely telling me what was happening and wringing their hands, Mark put his career on the line for David. It was an incredible gift.

"I hope this letter will help you to free David. It's all I could do."

"It is more than anyone else has done to help, Mark." I looked at the letter again, hardly daring to believe the support. "I'll give a copy of this to the IG at Spires Army Medical Center and to the inspector general of the army."

"Good. Maybe they'll help." Mark held out his hand. "Good luck, Lissa."

"Thanks." I shook his hand and hugged Julie. "God bless you for this!"

Shortly after Mark left, I called Max at the radio station and told him I couldn't do the children's program anymore because I had to go back to the States. Then I added, "Max, I'm looking for character witnesses for David. Witnesses who will write to our congressman so he knows that David is a man of competence and integrity. Could you ...?"

"Just give me his address, Lissa. I will most certainly do that. What the army is doing to David is outrageous! He's one of the finest doctors I've ever met!"

"Thank you, Max." I paused. "I'm not sure if David can be freed before the army destroys him. It's looking bad. But thank you for letting the Quito, Ecuador, station know about me, just in case ..." I sighed.

"God be with you, Lissa."

"Thank you. Good-bye, Max." My heart ached to leave the radio station. It had been such a pleasure to do something significant for the children of the Philippines. Now that phase of my life was over. Would I ever again have such an opportunity? I didn't know. But something in my heart felt empty, and I felt the answer was no.

13

OVER THE FENCE
(NOVEMBER)

T IME WAS RUNNING out. The children and I would fly out of the Philippines in two days. I'd sold the car and the fishing boat. The paperwork to ship our goods back to the States had been turned in. The suitcases were packed. The two weeks I'd allowed myself were almost up. All I needed now was to make reservations on a flight back to Oklahoma. As I reached for the phone, it began to ring.

"Mrs. McCloud?" It was a woman's voice.

"Yes."

"This is Major Buckley at the housing office. Could you please come over?"

"Is there a problem?"

"Yes. I need to speak with you." She sounded annoyed.

"I'll come right over." I needed to get this over quickly and make those reservations. It was already nearly ten in the morning.

A few minutes later I stood in Major Buckley's office, next door to the hospital. A tall, brown-haired woman sat behind the desk.

"Come in. You are Mrs. McCloud?"

"Yes. What do you need?"

"Mrs. McCloud, your husband does not have orders to go back to the States. You cannot leave the Philippines!"

My eyes met hers. "Watch me!"

"Now, listen to me! You cannot just have your things shipped back, and you cannot leave them here, because they will be stolen. You must stay with your household goods."

"Major Buckley, my maid, Marina, will be staying in our base house until our household goods are shipped. She will take care of our things and ensure they are not stolen."

"She will steal you blind!"

"No. She will not. I trust her far more than I trust the army. Look at what you're doing to my husband!" I was indignant. "Marina is trustworthy. I have arranged for her to sign for our shipment when the time comes. I want her left alone. Nobody is to bother her, do you understand?"

Major Buckley looked uncomfortable. "This is highly irregular, Mrs. McCloud!"

"You have a copy of David's power-of-attorney, which he gave me to use to have our things shipped. You have a signed and witnessed permission for Marina to stay with our household goods. I think that should be everything you need." I stood. "Will that be all?"

She frowned hard at me.

I stared back.

Her eyes fell. "Yes."

"Thank you." I walked out of the room.

As I left the office, I breathed a sigh of relief. Though I felt drained after meeting with Major Buckley, I still needed to pick up David's diploma and medical license, which were hanging on his office wall. I decided to fetch the documents before driving home. I could unwind later. There was so little time left before the children and I must fly out; I had to crowd as much as possible into each day.

The hospital loomed before me. I pulled the truck into the parking lot and I entered through the basement, then took the elevator up to radiology. Stepping into the hall, I walked toward Candy's desk.

"Mrs. McCloud!" she exclaimed, coming toward me. "How is Dr. McCloud?" Other staff members came out into the hall and gathered around me, their faces showing great concern. None of the Filipino doctors came forward—just those who served in the office or who worked as technicians.

"Candy, it's looking bad," I said. "The doctors at Spires are determined to destroy David. I'm trying to get him out of there, but it's going to take some time, I'm afraid."

Marlene, one of the radiology techs, burst into tears. "He is Job![8] He has done nothing wrong, yet he suffers for it. Oh, God, help him!" She put her hands over her face and turned away.

Others wiped tears or looked stony-faced at the floor.

"I need to get David's diploma and medical license from his office," I told Candy. "I'm taking the children back to the States. It's going to be a long battle, and I need to be with David while he goes through it. We're probably not coming back."

"Okay," she said. "And good luck."

Everything in David's office was as he had left it nearly two months before, with medical books on one corner of the desk, his pen lying next to them as though he would be right back to sign papers. I stood at the window and looked over the city, with its giant trees lining the main boulevards. It seemed like yesterday when I had first stood in his office. David's arm lay across my shoulders while he pointed out the various landmarks, smiled, and told me about his new job.

I wiped tears from my eyes and reached for his framed diploma and license. I tucked them under my arm and walked to the elevator.

Oh, no! Marge Aiken stood waiting for me in front of the elevator. I couldn't avoid her. I hesitated, unsure what to do. I wondered if someone had called her; there was no reason she could have known I was there, and she was obviously waiting for me. Her shoulders drooped and her hair was frazzled. She looked ill.

She didn't beat around the bush. "Lissa! I know what's happening to David, and you need to know that my husband is not doing this thing!"

I pushed the elevator button and said nothing, studying her out of the corner of my eye.

"You must listen to me! This is the work of Colonel Barnett, not my husband!"

The elevator door opened and I stepped inside. She followed me, and the door slid closed, shutting us in together. I pushed the button for the ground floor, and the elevator began to descend.

"Colonel Barnett's daughter told my daughter that her dad planned to become the commander of this hospital." She snorted. "As if he could! He's been spreading lies about Lem! He's accused him of all kinds of things. But I've heard that Colonel Barnett owns two warehouses and is shipping things to the States illegally. It's even been said that he's running drugs! I can't prove it, but I think it is true! He has way too much money for someone of his pay grade."

"Do you want me to talk with your husband about this?"

"No! Don't do that! But you need to know he's not doing anything to hurt David!"

The elevator door opened.

I stepped out, but Marge remained inside.

"Thank you for telling me, Marge. I'll keep it in mind."

As the elevator door slid shut between us, my last view of Marge was fixed in my mind. I will always remember her as I saw her in that moment: distraught, her hair messed up, and her face filled with anxiety.

My mind was suddenly swept by fear. Was Colonel Barnett *really* involved in drug smuggling? If so, then David and I were up against powers that threatened our lives even more than we had realized. How could I defend David?

My friends in the Philippines had warned me that fighting these men was not safe, that they could indeed have us killed. I had tried not to listen. Was David right in his insistence that I stay out of this battle? Was it truly a matter of life and death, even for me?

Then again, was Marge telling the truth? Or was this just an attempt to shift blame to Colonel Barnett?

Yes, Colonel Barnett was the one continuing the harassment, but the first attack had come from Colonel Lem Aiken. I would not let Marge sidetrack me. Still, my heart went out to her. I could see how worried she was. Poor woman. How sad that she had been drawn into this conflict ... a conflict created by corruption ... where none would come through unscathed.

Her accusations of Colonel Barnett being involved with drug-dealing haunted me—frightening me into a state of indecision over the coming battle. Was David right? Was it better if I stayed out of the fight for the sake of our children?

It was nearly time for the children to come home from their last day of school in the Philippines. I was finishing with the packing when the phone rang.

"Mrs. McCloud?"

"Yes."

"My name is Colonel Erickson. I command the Marines in the Philippines, and I work closely with Admiral Grady. My mother called me from California yesterday. She is in a Bible study with David's mom, and she heard what was happening. May I come over to your place and talk with you about this?"

"Yes!" I was stunned. How small is the circle of Christians! I thanked him and said I had time now, if he could come over. He said he would be right there.

I heard the clatter of shoes coming up the stairs. The children were home from school. I'd been trying to keep them out of this struggle, trying to create as normal an environment as possible. If they were to hear my conversation with Colonel Erickson, they would be frightened.

"Hi, Mom!" Ryan burst into the house with Suzanna on his heels.

"Mom! Look what I made today!" Suzanna held up a watercolor picture.

"Oh, it's beautiful!" I looked at the picture and asked her about it—watching her face while she talked and listening to Ryan's comments, too. I was glad to hear they had enjoyed their last day at school in the Philippines. They hadn't been at the school long enough to make deep friendships, so leaving wasn't an issue with them. They were eager to see their dad again.

"Cookies!" Marina announced, sticking her head around the kitchen doorway.

Both children dashed to the table and slid into their chairs for an after-school snack. Sitting next to them, I said, "Children, a colonel is coming over to talk to me in a little bit. When he comes, I want you to go up to your rooms and play for a while so we can talk. Okay?"

Ryan gave me a searching look. "Sure, Mom."

"Okay," Suzanna said. "Can Rosy come up with us?"

"Yes." Marina swung the toddler up on her lap and gave her a cookie.

An hour later, I opened the door to Colonel Erickson. He was tall and rugged looking, with tightly curled gray hair. I ushered him into the living room.

By now, having told it repeatedly, I had narrowed the account down to the basics. When he asked, I spelled it out with brutal directness. We spoke for about an hour, and he asked me many questions.

At the close of our conversation, Colonel Erickson said, "Mrs. McCloud, I am going to do everything I can to help you free David. I will be acting as your liaison with Admiral Grady. Here's my card. I will try to keep in close touch with you. Let me know when you have a phone in the States."

"I will."

"Mrs. McCloud, my prayers will be with you and David through this."

"Thank you." I was deeply touched by his support.

I walked with him to the doorway. As I passed the staircase to the bedrooms, I glimpsed sneakers and blue jeans disappearing up the stairs. Ryan had been listening. He probably knew most of what was happening, but it might ease his mind to ask questions. I'd talk with him later.

After Colonel Erickson left, I bowed my head and thanked God for all the help he was providing through all the good officers who had rallied behind us. Maybe, just maybe, David would be set free!

But would it be in time?

The next morning, the children and I left the Philippines. My last memory of our home there was of Marina's tear-stained face. Dear Marina ... my sister and friend ... she will always be the symbol of the Philippines to me. She embodied all the best of the Filipino people with her love, warmth, and sweet spirit. She hugged each of us tightly, as we hugged her and little Rosy. They had become our family. This was good-bye until we would meet in heaven. There were no dry eyes.

I was still thinking of Marina and Rosy when we boarded the plane. I would, of course, write to her. But I would miss her dreadfully. I found our seats. The children were assigned seats across the aisle from mine, midway down the plane. Each had brought a book, so we pulled them out of their backpacks and stowed the rest under the seats. I checked their seat belts to make sure they were on correctly.

"Put your books in the rack in front of you for take-off," I said.

"Okay, Mom." Ryan helped Suzanna put her book in the pocket in front of her and stowed his own where he could reach it later.

Taking my place across the aisle, I leaned back and relaxed. We were going to David. We were leaving behind the threats and the politics of the Philippine situation. That was a relief. But we were also leaving behind some very dear friends.

The plane rose through the dense clouds over the Philippines ... and flew into the heart of a thunderstorm. It bucked and dropped toward the ground. We were lifted off our seats. I held the armrests with all my strength. The children, safely fastened in their seats, did the same.

People began screaming ... and praying. Ryan and Suzanna sat frozen, their eyes wide with terror. I reached for Ryan's hand and gripped it tightly. On the other side, Suzanna's fingers were pressed into his forearm.

The plane caught an updraft and again began to climb. Then a second downdraft sucked the plane toward the earth, through lightning-streaked clouds.

As the plane fell, I cried out silently to God to help us. I remembered that Satan is called the "prince of the power of the air."[9] We were caught in his territory! I could not have spoken aloud in that moment, my throat was so tightly constricted. Again, the plane was caught up and held.

The smell of urine filled the cabin. Some of the passengers were emotionally falling apart. Screams and prayers sounded around us. But the children and I sat frozen into silence, our prayers thrown silently heavenward.

A third time, the plane plummeted. This time I could see the earth coming toward us. But just in time, the plane bucked and held. It rose through the clouds and fought its way into safe airspace.

A few minutes later, Ryan showed me his arm where Suzanna had held him. His skin was still indented from her grip.

The entire flight was bumpy, and we tensed at every downdraft. When we landed in Narita, the children began chanting softly in sing-song voices, "We're still alive! We're still alive!" The other passengers shouted and clapped. A cheer went up.

The plane taxied to a gate at the terminal. The cabin door opened and the pilot entered the aisle, his hair ruffled and fallen over one eye. The cabin erupted in applause.

Surely our God had protected us! I knew this was only the beginning of our time of great trials. But it was comforting to know that God was holding us in the palm of his hand, keeping us safe … even against a spirit world pitted against him and those who serve him.

14

BATTLE PLANS

David's narrative

I was relieved to see Lissa again, to know that the army could not separate us. Her love gives me courage. But I don't want her to get involved in this battle. It is too dangerous. The lead psychiatrist here, Colonel Black, told me Lissa's story about what happened in the Philippines is bizarre. She is basing everything on her own judgment of what is believable.

I think she wants to go after Lissa, too. It scares me. What if she gets hold of Lissa? What if she manages to take our children away from us? I want Lissa to stay out of this! I think she will, because she always does what I ask. But she is so full of fire and life, I never know for sure what she will do. If anyone would charge hell with a bucket of water, Lissa would! I pray that she will be safe.

Mom and Dad came out when Lissa left. Though the psychiatrists here have tried to keep me from eating, Mom and Dad have been insistent. Some days the orders are for me to stay on the psychiatric ward. The psychiatrist writes that I've been "bad" and must be punished by staying here. But Mom and Dad bring me food on those days. Other days, I'm supposedly "good" and am allowed off the ward. No rationale is given for these arbitrary rulings. It's very demeaning.

I've asked the psychiatrist when I'll be permitted to leave. The story changes from day to day. First I'll be released in "two or three days." Then, when two or three days have passed, the psychiatrist says, "Oh, in another week." There's never any reason given. The story always changes. I cannot trust the psychiatrists here. I just have to keep focused on Christ and trust him to deliver me from my enemies.

Lissa is due back here tomorrow. She's bringing the children. It will be so good to see them again! I have missed them terribly.

W E MET DAVID in the main lobby at Spires Army Medical Center.

"Daddy!" Suzanna squealed with joy, throwing herself into David's arms.

Ryan, always more reserved, walked up to his dad and slid into the curve of his side, leaning his head against his dad, while David's free arm came around his shoulders.

It was the first time the children had seen their dad in almost two months.

Leaning over the children, I kissed my husband. There were tears in his eyes. It was a precious moment.

Lewis and Ruth, David's parents, stood back, smiling, allowing us some time together. They had arrived in Oklahoma the day after I'd left, and had stayed until I could return with the children. They planned to leave for home the following day.

Both children wanted to talk at once, so we left the hospital lobby and went out to the sunny lawn, where David and the children could reconnect. After the long flight and drive, the children needed to run and play awhile.

While David played with the children, Lewis, Ruth, and I sat together at a picnic table and conferred.

"Lissa, I talked to the JAG here, but nobody wanted to help David," Lewis said. "They said they are too busy now. They gave me the name of an ex-JAG who works in town. A Mr. Goodman. They said you'd have to work with him." He handed me a piece of paper.

"Dad, David told me to bring the children up here, then to stay out of this fight," I said. "I'll talk to this lawyer, but I don't know what else to do. I've spoken with Admiral Grady's staff, and I think the admiral might intervene. It's the best I can do."

"Lissa, we don't know how to help David," Lewis said. "We aren't knowledgeable enough, and we will be too far away. But if you will take on his defense, we'll stand with you—and back you up all the way. We'll help pay for the lawyer. I know you are running short on money with all this travel to and from the Philippines. But something must be done! We think you have what it takes to get David out of this."

"But ..." My heart began to pound. What they were asking was impossible! This was the *army!* I would be facing an enemy armed with resources beyond imagination.

I had hoped that Lewis would have found a JAG officer to help. The battle was too much for me. I had never studied law! I was small and unimpressive. My voice sounded so young that when strangers phoned, they usually asked, "Is your mommy home?" And in the military, I had absolutely no clout. I did not want to head up this fight!

Then I looked at David: the light in his eyes as he played with the children, the smile of joy when he looked at me. All I had was an undying love and loyalty for him. Was it enough? I felt the world descend on my shoulders. I could not live with myself if I didn't fight to free him. It was indeed up to me to lead the battle for his deliverance. Though I didn't feel adequate, God had placed the assignment squarely on me. I was terribly frightened and insecure, but I had no choice. I would fight with every ounce of strength.

I struggled with the church teachings of a lifetime—teachings that said I must obey my husband, no matter what. David had said to stay out of the battle. He was trying to protect me. But *should* I stay out of it?

Words of Christian women echoed in my brain: "If we just obey our husbands, God honors that. We have to trust that God's ways are not our own, that he will make all things work out for good if we are obedient to our husbands."

Then words from a favorite Agatha Christie novel came into my mind: "We are not put into this world ... to avoid danger when an innocent fellow creature's life is at stake."[10]

She was right.

At times, God asks us to step outside our box to serve him. With God, there are no "one size fits all" formulas. We need to listen to the still small voice, the voice of the Holy Spirit, who guides us individually on the path we should follow, though it may not fit our preconceived theories or the teachings of some wise, earthly leader. This was one of those times.

So I set aside those teachings. What David and I faced was exceptional. We were a team, and my leader was under attack. This was no time for me to sit by, claiming obedience, while wicked people tried to destroy my husband!

"Okay," I said. "I'll do it." With that decision, I stepped into the swamp from my nightmare. "But you must organize prayer chains for me. You must rally other Christians to stand behind me in prayer. I cannot do this without God's help!"

Lewis and Ruth looked relieved.

If anyone had taken a photo of us, labeling it "David's Defense Team," no one would have given us a chance. There we sat—none of us taller than five-foot-three—planning to take on the United States Army!

But we had one great advantage: Our God was and is much bigger than the United States Army, much more powerful, and much more dangerous. Our trust was not in ourselves, but in our God. He stood behind us, backing us all the way. And he had a plan.

"I think the first thing to do is to get a copy of David's medical records so we can prove what those psychiatrists are doing to him," I told Lewis. "I will ask for them this afternoon."

"That sounds like a good plan. From what David tells me, they're putting him through brainwashing."

"That's what it sounds like." I shook my head. "I would never have dreamed that the United States Army would do this to their own troops! I thought only Russia and China engaged in this kind of abuse!"

Lewis, a patriotic World War II veteran, bowed his head. I could see the struggle on his face.

Ruth lifted her chin and looked into the distance, stoic and determined. She was quiet and calm, but underneath her gentleness there was steel. From the moment we met, she had been my best friend. I knew I could count on her to pray for us continually and to rally others to prayer—the key to unlocking God's power.

After we visited a little longer, I excused myself and went up to the psychiatric ward. At the nurses' desk, I asked to see the chief of psychiatry.

"That would be Colonel Black," the nurse said. "Just a minute while I call her office." She spoke briefly on the phone, then directed me down the hallway to the at a door at the end.

I knocked.

"Come in."

I entered. "Colonel Black?"

"Yes?" she said abruptly, looking up from her work. A large woman, her hair was short and red, with flecks of white flaring in wings framing her face. She did not invite me to sit.

"I would like to have a copy of my husband's medical records." I stood just inside the door, not wanting to get close to this woman.

"No." She stared across at me. I could feel her hostility.

"I am his wife. I am entitled to see those records."

"No. You may not have them. They are confidential."

"You *will* give them to me!"

"No."

"Yes. You *will*." I stepped back and opened the door, not taking my eyes from this formidable enemy. Black was her name, and black was her heart. But I would not let her block me.

Shutting the door quietly, I found that my hands were shaking. I breathed deeply and headed toward the elevator. There was someone I must see. At the hospital entry level, I turned toward Major Duggan's office, the inspector general. His door stood open. I knocked on the doorframe.

"Mrs. McCloud! Come in!" He smiled and stood.

"Thank you, Major Duggan."

"Ben. Please call me Ben."

"Okay." I smiled.

"Have a seat." He motioned to a chair.

"Thanks." I sat back and looked across the desk at the IG. "Ben, I asked Colonel Black for David's medical records, and she refused to give me a copy."

Ben's face darkened. "She *has* to give them to you! The Freedom of Information Act requires it!" He stood. "Mrs. McCloud, come by my office tomorrow. I will make sure you have a copy of those records."

"Thank you, Ben. Somehow I knew I could count on you." I left his office and rejoined the family in the garden. Ben would be another valuable ally, I thought, chalking up his name on my list. And by tomorrow, I would have proof of what was being done to David.

David's parents left for California the next morning, but not before I stopped by Ben Duggan's office.

"Mrs. McCloud, here are David's medical records." He handed me a thick manila envelope. "They didn't want to hand them over, but I gave them no choice."

"Ben, you are one fine officer," I said. "Thank you!"

"My pleasure, ma'am." He smiled. "Let me know if I can do anything else."

"I will." I turned, then looked back over my shoulder. "Ben, you're a good man."

His face glowed. "Thank you."

David's parents were waiting with the children in the lobby. I sat next to Ruth. "I've got the medical records. When I've had a chance to look them over, I'll call you."

Lewis nodded. "We need to be going. We're going up to say good-bye to David first."

"Okay. If he's free to leave the ward today, tell him to come back down with you." I wasn't going to take the children to the psychiatric ward. They would find it too traumatic.

A few minutes later, Lewis and Ruth returned with David. He was wearing blue jeans and a pullover shirt instead of the psychiatric ward outfit. He was carrying a duffel bag. Could he be free? No, that would be too much to ask.

We exchanged hugs with his parents and said our good-byes, waving as they walked to their rental car.

It was the first Friday in November.

David put his arm across my shoulder. "The doctors have given me permission to leave the hospital for the weekend to help you and the children find a house."

"Oh, David!" This was Ben Duggan's doing, I felt sure.

"Let's get out of here." He took my hand and scooped up Suzanna.

For the first time since September, we were a family. Tonight I would again sleep in my husband's arms.

15

ESTABLISHING A BASE

AUTUMN LEAVES BLEW though the air in swirls of gold and red. The sun shone brightly, and our spirits were optimistic. We found a real estate office near the post. An agent ushered us into his office, asking how he could help.

"We're looking for a small, month-to-month rental for our stay in Oklahoma," David said. "I'm in the military and do not know how long we will be here."

"Sure," the agent said. "Here is a list of the possibilities near the fort." He reached into his desk and pulled out a list. "Would you like me to come with you?"

"No, thank you," I said. "We'll drive around and look at some, then call you."

By that afternoon, we had found a small, red brick house we liked in the little town of Elmsville, about five miles from Fort Hardin. We had no furniture yet, so we rented a few things to hold us until our household goods arrived. It was a quiet neighborhood with large lawns, backyard gardens, and young families like ours. It felt comfortable.

Sunday we found a church where we could worship together. The people were friendly, and our children liked it. My heart was glad. But the effort to meet people exhausted me. I'd lost so much weight so quickly, I had very little strength. The struggle to move the family back to the States, the emotional battles, and the prospect of future battles had completely drained me.

Late on Sunday, after a long nap, I opened the envelope with David's hospital records. I could hear David and the children talking in the other room. Sitting there in bed, I studied the hand-written pages. What I read infuriated me. The doctors had twisted his words unbelievably, making David sound almost incoherent. Phrases leaped off the page:

"Patient won't mix socially. Stays in room reading Bible. Hyper-religious ..."
"Confine to ward. Patient encouraged not to eat ..."
"Patient believes in something called the 'rapture' ... Delusional ..."
"Patient is losing weight. Sign of depression ..."
"Patient thinks his commanding officer put him here to discredit him ... Paranoid schizophrenia ..."
"Patient doesn't trust doctors. Further indication of paranoia ..."
"Irrational story about situation at last assignment ..."
"Considering electric shock treatment to stop delusions ..."
"Confine to ward. Patient encouraged not to eat ..."

No tests had been ordered to explore why David was feverish, why his bilirubin was high, or why he was yellow.

It was a hatchet job. Clearly, the resident psychiatrist was sadistic! It was all there in black and white. I wept. How could I hope to extricate David from this morass of lies? "Oh, God! Help me! Help me!" I whispered.

I dropped the papers onto the bed and put my hands over my face, tears slipping through my fingers and down my neck. The enormity of the task ahead overwhelmed me. What could I do? Where could I begin? These enemies were so many and so powerful!

From the depths of my memory, words bubbled to the surface, words repeated many times in the Louis L'Amour novels I had read. His standard advice: "When outnumbered, always attack."

I was most certainly outnumbered! So what could I do to attack? I dried my eyes, reached for a piece of paper, and began brainstorming. A Bible verse came to mind:

> In a certain town there was a judge who neither feared God nor cared about men. And there was a widow in that town who kept coming to him with the plea, "Grant me justice against my adversary." For some time he refused. But finally he said to himself, "Even though I don't fear God or care about men, yet because this widow keeps bothering me, I will see that she gets justice, so that she won't eventually wear me out with her coming."
>
> —Luke 18:2-5

Yes, that is exactly what I will do, I thought. I will keep bothering the people in command ... and in government ... until they free David. I will give them no rest!

I listed all the people involved in this case and began planning the attack. It would need to be a battle fought without David's knowledge, for he remained determined to protect me from the people who were trying to destroy him.

Several of my friends had warned me my life would be in danger if I fought the military establishment. The army, they said, would even bug our phones. None of my Christian friends in the Philippines had trusted the military there. They had seen too much corruption.

But we are back in the States now, I thought. This is *America!* Regardless of what others say, I believe in this country ... in our Constitution that guarantees our freedom ... in our laws. These military doctors may think they can get away with what they're doing to David, but I have the law on my side. Surely that counts for something! I will not listen to those who are afraid to stand up to abuse. This is *my* country, and I will use every avenue to achieve justice for David.

Yes, I knew those psychiatrists were dangerous, unethical, and intimidating. Who could fight against them when their diagnosis, treatments, and tactics kept changing?

Yes, I knew there were some bad apples in the military. No element of society is immune from corruption. But there were many more good people—like Major Ben Duggan, Colonel Erickson, Admiral Grady, Major Mark Ralston, and Sergeant Gerald Smith—who would help me.

With all the bright lights of a Department of the Army inspector general investigation shining on this situation, I would probably be safe. But if not, I did not fear death. I had faced it, in other situations, twice already, and Jesus had been with me in those moments of danger. I knew that if I died, it would be for a cause I couldn't ignore, and the children would have a good guardian: David's brother.

So I wrote out my battle plan and prayed over it, committing my efforts and my safety to God. Then I folded it, placed it in my Bible, and went out to join my family.

David's narrative:

It was so good to be with my family again! I feel so much better, knowing they are here ... and safe. But it was difficult to go back to the psychiatric ward. The psychiatrist gave me a short time with my family. I'll be permitted to join them on weekends. But I have to stay at the hospital during the week.

Fortunately, the psychiatrists have stopped trying to withhold food from me. My family has seen to it that I have what I need. They've done an end run around that tactic. But the psychiatrists are still trying to play mind games by telling me first one thing, then another, about when I will be released. Today I was told they would release me to go home at night if I will take Haldol, a powerful antipsychotic drug. I don't think that is a good idea at all. But I don't know how long I can hold out against them; the temptation to be with my family is great. I need to resist this coercion!

The children and I would need new, warmer clothes for the Oklahoma fall and winter. I felt sure we would be here at least that long. No matter what the psychiatrists were telling David about letting him go soon, I saw through their tactics. They were trying to break him, and their promises were empty. This would be a long, ugly battle.

"Okay, Ryan and Suzanna, let's go shopping!" I said early Monday morning. There was a larger town twenty miles from Elmsville—a town with a mall.

On the way, the children and I discussed schooling. "I think we should do home school again this year," I said. "What do you think?"

"How long will we be here?" Ryan wanted to know. He was riding shotgun.

"I don't know, honey. That's why I'm thinking it might be best to just keep going with our own curriculum."

"I like that," Suzanna said from the back seat. New environments frightened her.

"How about you, Ryan?"

"Okay, I guess." Ryan liked socializing and sports. "There's some kids in the neighborhood I can hang out with in the afternoons and on the weekends."

"If you are okay with it, then we'll start classes tomorrow," I said. "I bought some books in the Philippines just in case."

We found what we needed at the mall: winter coats, jeans, warm sweaters, closed-toe shoes and boots for the snow, and some dress clothes for church. Afterward, we ate lunch in the food court under a skylight, with palm plants artfully scattered through the area.

"Do they have a pet store here?" Ryan asked. He always wanted to see the animals in the mall.

"Let's look at the directory."

"Yes!" Ryan pointed to the map. "There's the pet store! Let's go!" He was off, Suzanna close behind him.

I smiled and followed.

Cats, rabbits, guinea pigs, fish, puppies ... We looked at them all. But Ryan kept returning to look at an adorable beagle puppy with big, sad eyes.

"Can I hold him?" Ryan asked.

Sensing a sale, the store attendant stepped over. "Why don't you take him into the side room and see how you get along?"

"Great!"

The puppy was perfect. I could see that the children loved him. This would be a way to distract them from the difficulties our family was facing. Our new house had a large, fenced back yard, perfect for pets. Yes, we would buy the puppy. Besides, the children had already named him Freckles.

Adding dog food and a couple of feeding bowls to our bags, we headed back to the car. This time, both children sat in the back with Freckles. Delight filled the air. It was a foregone conclusion that the puppy would sleep at the foot of Ryan's bed.

I smiled. Things were starting to come together.

On the way home, we passed a piano store. My piano was still in the Philippines, and I knew there would be days ahead when I would need to work out my frustrations. We stopped and I picked out a small piano to rent until my own was shipped to us. Now I too would have a way to ease some of the pain and fury of future battles. We arrived back home in good spirits.

The next morning we resumed our home-schooling. By noon, lessons were done and the children could watch TV or play with Freckles.

But I had calls to make, a campaign to start. This would become the daily routine: school first, then I'd make calls, searching for people to help David, hounding people in authority, urging them to help.

Yes, it would be stressful. But having a routine would help me survive. I could compartmentalize my days, allowing only an hour each afternoon for the stressful phone calls. I knew I'd need to pace myself, for the battle would be long.

ESTABLISHING A BASE

That first day, I made an appointment with Mr. Goodman, the attorney recommended by the JAG. He had an opening that afternoon, so I went right over, leaving Ryan in charge of Suzanna and the puppy. Mr. Goodman's office was in a tall, red brick building with white trim and regal columns at the door. A few leaves still clung to the branches of the oak tree outside, and the small lawn sandwiched between the building and the sidewalk was sprinkled with autumn's gold.

I walked into the building with its tall doors. It was dark inside and a little musty. One wall was covered with leather-bound books. Carved wooden chairs with red leather cushions stood next to a large desk, behind which sat a cheerful, plump woman. A brass nameplate on her desk announced she was the receptionist.

"May I help you?" Her eyes crinkled at the corners, and her face lit in a comfortable smile.

"I'm here to see Mr. Goodman."

"Just a moment," she waved to a seat and disappeared through a door. She returned promptly and said, "Mr. Goodman will see you now."

"Mrs. McCloud!" a genial voice called.

A plump, middle-aged man came forward to greet me. I wondered if the receptionist was his wife. They were much alike in manner and expression, the way two people become after many years of marriage.

Nervously, I sat on the chair next to Mr. Goodman's desk. The scent of lemon oil rose from the polished wood surface.

"What may I do for you, Mrs. McCloud?"

I took a deep breath and plunged into my account of what had happened. I could see by his expression that Mr. Goodman was withholding judgment. I handed him a copy of Major Mark Ralston's letter. "I know it is an incredible story, Mr. Goodman. But here is some verification of the command situation in the Philippines."

He put on his reading glasses and perused the letter, his eyebrows rising. When he was finished, he put the paper on his desk and looked over his glasses at me.

"This is not the only witness to what has happened to my husband," I said. "Admiral Grady's staff is standing by to help us, too. I don't have anything yet in writing, but I have been in contact with the IG of the Philippines, with Admiral Grady's personal lawyer, and the army surgeon general of the Philippines. Colonel Erickson, the commander of the Marines there, is acting as my liaison with the admiral. I have been told that the command agrees that David is facing psychiatric retaliation for his reporting of illegal activities."

"What would you like me to do for you, Mrs. McCloud?"

"I would like you to help me get David out of the military with his medical license intact."

"That I can probably do," he said. "I will need to meet with your husband to see for myself that he is mentally competent. Then I will set up an appointment with the deputy commander of clinical services, Colonel Austin. You and I will present Dr. McCloud's case, and we will see where to go from there."

"Good." I sighed with relief. "I will be trying to round up other help, too. I will want to run things by you to make sure I'm handling this correctly. Is that okay?"

"Yes. That would be a good idea. I need to be kept in the loop."

Back in my car, I leaned my head on the steering wheel and sighed. Now we had some legal help, even if he didn't look energetic.

Returning home, I gathered Ryan's science and math books and called the children. "Let's go over to see Dad." I was no good at science and math. David would have to help with those two subjects.

At the hospital, I left the children in the lobby and went up to David's room. "It's dinner time," I said. "The children are waiting downstairs for us. Afterward, maybe you could help Ryan with some of his homework."

David's arms came around me, and I buried my head in his shoulder. Somehow, I thought, I have to keep this family intact.

In that moment, I decided that wherever David was, that was home. If he were confined to the hospital, then our home would be the lobby, the cafeteria, and the hospital garden. We would play on the garden lawn. We would spread out Ryan's books on the lobby table and pretend it was our living room. We would gather as a family in the cafeteria, hold hands and pray, and discuss the day's activities while we ate. We would block out the world and exist in our own small sphere. In my mind, I called it "Operation Family."

While the army was trying to tear us apart, I'd be running my own op to counter them, and I'd be doing it right in their own facility.

Let people stare! Let them wonder! I didn't care. These people had captured the love of my life, and I would not be separated from him.

16

ALLIES

THE FOLLOWING AFTERNOON, I called one of David's former commanding officers, Colonel Andrew Leigh. He had retired the year before and had moved back to his ranch in Arizona. His wife, Beth, was a very dear friend.

Beth answered the phone.

"Hi, Beth, this is Lissa."

"Lissa! Where are you? Last I heard, you were in the Philippines!"

"We're in Oklahoma. Something bad has happened, and I need to talk with Andy. Is he around?"

"Let me get him. You will tell me what's going on after you talk with him?"

"Yes."

Andy came on the line. "Lissa, what's up?"

"Hi, Andy. I need your help. David's commanders in the Philippines, Colonel Aiken and Colonel Barnett, tried to get him involved in illegal activities. When he refused, they began threatening him, so he reported it to the IG. Then his commanders had him locked up in the psychiatric ward at Spires Army Medical Center, and I can't get him out. They're saying he's mentally ill. But it isn't true."

Andy was silent for a moment. "Lissa, what can I do to help?"

"Please, Andy, could you write to the IG at Spires and support David?"

"Yes. I can do that. What's his address?"

I pulled out Major Ben Duggan's card and gave Andy the address.

"I'll get right on it, Lissa."

He asked a few more questions, then handed the phone back to Beth.

It was exhausting to tell her all the details, but it was also a relief. She was a good friend and she understood.

A few days later, Major Ben Duggan called. "Mrs. McCloud, I just received a letter of support for David from one of his former commanding officers, Colonel Leigh. It's very helpful. I'll make a copy for you. Could you stop by my office soon?"

"I'll be there this afternoon. Thank you, Ben."

That afternoon, I stopped by Ben's office. Standing by his desk, I read what Andy had written. It was a strong defense. Phrases leaped out at me:

> "I always knew him to be exceedingly bright, honest, and reliable. His personal faith and his intellect made him a very capable intern and medical corps officer. His performance and behavior was above reproach ... an acute psychotic episode stretches my credulity ... I would alert you to the fact that he may well be a more capable physician than either his Philippine commander or DCCS ..."

Yes. It was a good letter. It would help.

I remembered the first time I had met Colonel Leigh. It was at a department barbeque on the beach. A tall, handsome man, he was wearing a baseball cap and flipping hamburgers on a grill when David and I arrived with the children. I remembered how Colonel Leigh looked up and studied me. I'd wondered if he thought I'd support David's residency training and the time commitments required of a physician. I hoped now that he felt I was proving my worth to my husband.

I looked up at Ben. He was smiling.

"You've got some solid support there, Mrs. McCloud. It is significant that a former commanding officer would take a stand like this for your husband. It speaks volumes."

I grimaced. "Ben, everyone who knows David knows that this situation at Spires is based on lies."

Ben nodded thoughtfully.

"Thanks for the copy, Ben. I'll see you later." I walked out of his office and joined the family. I handed the letter to David and saw hope light up his face. I needed to gather more such testimony to support him.

The next day I pulled out Colonel Duffy's list of people who might help. I was surprised to see our neighbor from Fort Duran, Colonel Calloway, on the list. I dialed his number.

"Hello?" said a deep voice.

"Colonel Calloway, this is Lissa McCloud."

"Lissa! It's good to hear from you! What's going on?"

"Colonel, we're having a problem. Colonel Aiken and Colonel Barnett tried to get David to alter time cards and do other illegal stuff, and he said no. Then they threatened him ... and us ... so David reported them to the Department of the Army inspector general. To discredit him, the commanders had him admitted involuntarily to Spires Army Medical Center's psychiatric ward. I can't get him out!"

Colonel Calloway swore bitterly.

"Sir, I was wondering if you were aware of what was going on at Owen Hospital, since you were one of the commanding officers?"

Silence. "Lissa, I retired early to get away from that situation. I knew about the time cards and a lot of other illegal activity, and I tried to get it stopped. But Colonel Aiken threatened me, too."

"Can you help us?"

"What do you need, Lissa?"

"I need a letter of recommendation for David, and a letter telling about the illegal activities there."

Silence. I could tell he wasn't happy about my request.

"Okay," he said finally—and with conviction. "I'll do it. What's your address?"

"Thank you so much, Colonel Calloway!" I gave him our information.

"I'll do what I can, Lissa. How is David holding up?"

"He seems to be doing fine, now that I've brought the kids back to the States and have found a place to live nearby. How are you and Mary?"

"We're fine. I'm administering a civilian hospital here in Florida. I miss the Philippines, but it's good to be back where the law is respected."

"Tell Mary hi for me, and thank you again for your help."

"I'll get something in the mail for you today." He paused. "And Lissa?"

"Yes?"

"Good luck."

"Thanks."

The letter from Colonel Calloway arrived Saturday:

To whom it may concern:

This letter is written to provide information pertaining to the duty performance of Major (Dr.) David McCloud and also my knowledge and beliefs about the operations at Owen Army Hospital.

I was Deputy Commander of Administration at the MEDDAC Philippines for two years, serving at the same time as Dr. McCloud. The hospital was staffed by civilians (over 70%). It was not located on a secure military base and was adjacent to the highest crime area of Manila. Although the U.S. Army Health Services Command claimed that all hospitals within its command were accredited by the Joint Commission on Accreditation of Healthcare Organizations (JCAHO), this hospital was not.

Major McCloud arrived in the Philippines in the summer of my last year there. He came directly from his residency program and was assigned as the Chief of Radiology. As happens so frequently in the AMEDD, he was superbly trained in his medical specialty but completely untrained to be a leader/manager of a large complex department. He attempted to overcome his administrative shortcomings by working extremely hard and demonstrating an honest, true concern to provide the best possible medical care—with no military office staff. This staffing deficiency was typical of almost all clinical departments in the hospital and could not be corrected. At no time did I ever observe any inappropriate behavior. There were no patient complaints and patient care was far superior than that provided under the prior department chief. Major McCloud was a hard-working, concerned young officer.

During my two years in the Philippines, my perception of the overall environment was that corruption was an accepted way of life in that society. I believe this attitude existed among many members of the hospital staff, both clinical and administrative. I identified and attempted to correct numerous deficiencies, which resulted in saving over $4 million. All this information is on file at the Medical Command in Hawaii in the offices of the Inspector General and the Staff Judge Advocate. I believe these deficiencies probably existed from the date the army assumed responsibility for the hospital, and that no one would like to answer why they existed for so long. I do not feel I was supported by my commander and was left alone to implement corrective action. The commander wanted to be the "nice guy" and did not want to be responsible for upsetting anyone. My beliefs and frustrations led me to decide to retire from active duty after 25 years service. I could not, in good conscience, tolerate another year, though it meant giving up a pay raise at year 26 and therefore, over $300 per month for the rest of my life.

My commander, after a trip to our headquarters, informed me I had better not rock the boat too much (whistle-blow) or I would have problems finding a job after retirement. During my last few months in the Philippines, I was forced to administratively fight to protect my professional reputation and I believe I was "set up" by the commander to take the fall for his shortcomings. These efforts failed, and to a degree I have been able to protect myself. Upon retirement, I was awarded my second Legion of Merit.

After my departure, the command climate at the MEDDAC Philippines was investigated and as a result, the commander was removed. Although not a formal relief, it was in reality a de facto relief for cause.

Major McCloud is a very ethical, idealistic officer with the highest professional standards, and the environment he was placed into had an unfair impact on himself and his family.

Colonel (Ret.) Calloway

Ah! Colonel Calloway had also reported the commander's illegal activities—and had left before the commander could retaliate. Good. That report was on record. But why hadn't the IG moved to arrest Colonel Aiken? The entire high command in the Philippines knew of his corruption!

Colonel Calloway's letter of recommendation, sent in addition to this one, painted a glowing picture of David's work. And he concluded by saying he would proudly hire David at any hospital he managed and would recommend him to any other hospital as well.

The afternoon I received his letters, I took copies to Major Ben Duggan, along with the letter from Mark Ralston. Ben's face was grim as he read the two accounts of corruption and threats at Owen Army Hospital.

Ben looked up. "Mrs. McCloud, may I share these with the hospital command?"

"Yes, I want them to know the truth about what's happening. Maybe it will help free David."

Ben nodded. "I hope it will."

But it didn't. Knowing there was an IG investigation, the Spires staff decided to stick to their story rather than risk discipline for their part in an illegal psychiatric confinement.

17

ENEMIES

A FEW DAYS later, while I was helping the children with their schoolwork, Mr. Goodman called. "Mrs. McCloud, I have met with your husband and can see that he is not mentally ill. I've made an appointment with Colonel Austin, the deputy commander of clinical services, for 10:15 tomorrow morning. Can you be there?"

"Yes. I've spoken with Colonel Austin once before, and he was not at all inclined to release David. But with the evidence piling up, he may be more open."

"I'll see you in the hospital lobby at ten o'clock and we'll go over a few things first."

"I'll be there." I returned to the table where Suzanna was working on her reading exercise. It was difficult to focus on the schoolwork when my mind was racing toward the meeting. But I forced myself to concentrate on what was right in front of me. Tomorrow would come soon enough.

The next morning, before leaving for the hospital, I assigned homework for the children and left Ryan in charge. At age twelve, he was focused enough to get his own work done. And if he couldn't get Suzanna to finish, they could play with the puppy and I'd help Suzanna later.

At the Spires lobby, I met Mr. Goodman.

"Mrs. McCloud, I want you to let me do most of the talking. I've dealt with Colonel Austin before. We know each other professionally. He may ask you a few questions. Answer them as briefly and concisely as possible."

"I'll do my best."

In Colonel Austin's office, Mr. Goodman got us through the preliminary greetings and had me sit next to the deputy commander's large desk. He pulled a chair up and sat facing our opponent.

"Colonel Austin," he said, "I am concerned about what is being done to Dr. McCloud here at this hospital. I have met with him and find him to be clear and direct in his testimony. He is definitely not mentally ill."

Colonel Austin's features hardened. "I think that is for our psychiatrists to determine."

"I would like to have Dr. McCloud examined by an outside psychiatrist with no ties to the military." Mr. Goodman said.

"No." Colonel Austin's eyes were cold.

"Dr. McCloud is an excellent radiologist. I've seen his evaluation from his commanders. At least let him go back to work in your radiology department reading X-rays."

"No."

For several minutes, Mr. Goodman tried to negotiate with Colonel Austin, but got nowhere.

Colonel Austin's chin rose. "I think you will find that our psychiatrists know what they are doing."

"Then why not allow an outside psychiatrist to confirm your diagnosis?" Mr. Goodman asked gently.

"We will determine for ourselves what his mental state is. Our methods of diagnosis and treatment are very enlightened."

Enlightened! I couldn't keep quiet. In as calm a voice as I could muster, I said, "Your 'enlightened' methods are highly illegal, Colonel!"

Mr. Goodman nudged me and I shut up, holding back the words that wanted to spill out.

"Colonel, I know that your methods here are to tear a patient down and then rebuild him," Mr. Goodman said. "I've seen it many times before. But I do not think that treatment is warranted in this case. Dr. McCloud is mentally fit and should be put back to work."

Colonel Austin would not yield; we were getting nowhere. Finally, we left the colonel and returned to the lobby. As soon as we had cleared the hall, Mr. Goodman whispered, "These people are like the Mafia!" He shook his head. "You must be very careful, Mrs. McCloud. And keep me informed if you have any new evidence I can use."

I had given him every piece of evidence so far, and he was convinced of the military's retaliation against David. "I have a few more calls to make," I said. "Lt. Colonel Ingermann, the former chief of resource management at Owen Army Hospital, is in Washington, D.C. now. The surgeon general in the Philippines gave me his number and said he will probably help us. I'll call you if he does."

"Good," he said. "Please be careful, Mrs. McCloud."

I headed for Major Ben Duggan's office to report our conversation with Colonel Austin. I knew Ben was conducting his own investigation, and I wanted to get the words on record as soon as possible. He would be reporting everything to the Department of the Army inspector general.

Brian Newall, David's JAG friend, urged me to document all conversations as they happened, for they constituted legal evidence. Telling Ben now would keep him in the loop, and he could ask his own questions, getting first-hand evidence.

After speaking with Ben, I went out to the car and wrote the conversation on a legal pad and put the date and time at the top. I would later type it up and put it in my files. This case would be thoroughly documented, should it ever come to trial.

The next afternoon I received a phone call from Colonel Erickson, reporting on Admiral Grady's actions.

"Admiral Grady called the surgeon general of the army and warned him that David was being retaliated against and urged action to free him. But the surgeon general warned him to stay out of it—that interference would be seen as 'undue command influence' and could have negative results for David. The admiral can do nothing more. I'm sorry." Colonel Erickson sounded defeated.

I hung up the phone in shock. Knowing that Admiral Grady was on our side had been such a great hope! Now there would be no help from that source.

For the first time, I utterly collapsed. I slid off the bed and sat on the floor, my hands over my eyes, engulfed in tears. "God, where are you? Where are you?" I whispered. "I can't bear this!"

I could barely breathe through the sobs. Where could I go from here?

A knock sounded on my bedroom door. "Mommy?"

It was Suzanna. I tried to pull myself together and answer calmly. "Yes?"

"Can I get the mail this time?"

"Yes, honey."

I heard running footsteps and the front door open and slam closed. I went into the bathroom and splashed cold water on my face, then powdered my nose to hide the worst of the damage.

There was the knock again.

"Come in."

"Here's the mail, Mommy!"

"Just put it on the bed, honey."

I heard the letters land on the bedspread, and Suzanna went back out, shutting the door. I thumbed through the pile. Oh, good—a letter from my spiritual mother. I opened it and sat on the edge of the bed to read. It was a letter of encouragement, assuring me of their prayers. At the end, Mom had written out a Bible verse:

"For I know the plans I have for you," declares the Lord, "plans to prosper you and not to harm you, plans to give you hope and a future."
—Jeremiah 29:11

Though my heart was sore and beaten down, those words gave me courage. It did not seem like we had a future, but I knew that God loved us, and I clung to that verse.

In the months to come, each time a crushing event happened—and only at those times—I would receive a letter from a friend quoting that particular verse. The letters were all mailed days before the bottom dropped out of my world. They were always there—right on time. That verse became the buoy God used to lift me out of despair, the beacon to remind me of his presence and power, the pledge to let me know he would deliver us. For there was no way any person could have planned for that verse to arrive at the precise moment it was needed.

It was a God-thing. And I was comforted.

18

SABOTAGE

David's narrative:

I hate being separated from my family. Being home for the weekends
isn't enough. The psychiatric ward is a frightening place. I want out!
I was assigned work to do during the day: filing books in the hospital
library. It's humiliating. The psychiatrists have told me they will let me
go home after work every day if I agree to take Haldol. It's coercion.
But I've agreed to take it. I need my family. I can only hope and pray
that this drug won't mess me up too much.

WHEN DAVID TOLD me he had agreed to take Haldol, the
antipsychotic drug the doctors had been pushing him to
take, I was beside myself. He *couldn't* cave in like that! Then
I remembered the open elevator shaft next to his room. It had remained
open since he had been assigned that room, though I had never seen
any workmen around it. My stomach sank as I realized the implications
of his giving in. He was reaching the end of his emotional endurance.

Even if we had known then what we know now about Haldol, I still
don't think David could have held out. He was emotionally drained.

We did not realize Haldol was a mind-altering, addictive drug. It was
used in hypnosis and to sedate patients. Once started on it, many were
unable to drop it without serious mental repercussions. The psychiatrists
knew that, but we did not. We did not know that this was their way to
gain control over David, though I suspected as much. And though he
began taking Haldol, the psychiatrists still did not release him. They had
lied. Again.

I couldn't bear it.

By now, I had contacted our senator. She had written to the military liaison, demanding an explanation of their treatment of David and suggesting they should release him. But the military ignored our senator's request. This was getting serious, for the military was supposed to obey Congress. Now they had defied both a senator and a congressman.

I had been communicating weekly with our congressman in California, Representative Carl Newton. His aide, Sandi Paulson, was my contact. I called Sandi and told her what was happening.

Sandi was distressed. "Mr. Newton wrote to the military liaison and told him of the situation and said David should be *awarded a medal*, not locked up in the psychiatric ward! That should have been enough to free your husband, Lissa. But the commander at Spires is ignoring the congressional intervention. So Mr. Newton said to give you this phone number. It is for the Congressional Subcommittee on National Security, International Relations & Criminal Justice."

I took the number.

"Lissa, very few people are given this number. It is reserved for extreme circumstances, such as this one. Call them. Your contact's name will be Paul Gambol."

"Thank you, Sandi."

"Keep us informed!"

The next morning, before the children's classes, I called Paul Gambol at National Security. After I sketched the problem, he asked many questions.

Finally he said, "Mrs. McCloud, we will help you. But you need to know that things will get worse for your husband once the psychiatrists know that we are involved. They will try to break him in order to win. You must insist on being at each doctor appointment to ensure David's safety."

"I'll try." Remembering the cold, hard eyes of Colonel Black, I wasn't sure this would work. But I would at least ask.

"Good. Keep me informed about the situation."

I felt hopeful. Maybe, just maybe there would be some action now.

The next afternoon, I again approached Colonel Black's office. Taking a deep breath, I knocked.

"Come in," she called abruptly.

My heart pounded as I stepped inside, but I tried not to show my fear.

"Oh. It's you." She frowned.

"Colonel Black, our congressman has contacted the Congressional Subcommittee on National Security, International Relations & Criminal Justice on David's behalf. They will be investigating this situation. My contact at National Security has told me that I must be present every time you meet with my husband."

She stared at me. Finally she squinted and said coldly, "No. You may not be present. Not unless you come in as a patient, too."

Our eyes locked. She was a devil! My going into a meeting as a patient would discredit my testimony, and it would put my life under her control and in jeopardy. Worse, it would endanger my children, for she could then say whatever she wanted about me—and order them removed from my care. This was why David wanted me to stay out of the battle. He knew the potential danger to our family from these wicked people.

I walked out the door before the words welling up inside me could escape. Walking swiftly to the elevator, I headed for Ben Duggan's office.

"Mrs. McCloud, come in!" Ben said cheerfully.

"What's up?"

"My congressman has put me in touch with the Congressional Subcommittee on National Security, International Relations & Criminal Justice."

Ben's eyebrows rose.

"My contact at National Security said the psychiatrists will turn up the heat and try to break David once they are aware of their investigation, and that I need to be at each session to protect him. But Colonel Black will not allow that ... unless I agree to put myself under her power as a patient. I will *never* do that! She is unscrupulous and dangerous."

Ben studied me closely, his face grim. "Wait here. Mrs. McCloud. I'll go speak with her."

"Thank you, Ben."

Ten minutes later, he was back.

"I'm sorry, Mrs. McCloud. I spoke with Colonel Black and pointed out the seriousness of National Security's involvement and request, but she wouldn't yield. She said the only way she would allow you into the sessions with your husband would be if you were to come in as a patient."

"That isn't going to happen," I said. "I'm not sure how to protect David from her. But I absolutely do not trust her." I paused, my mind exploring possibilities. "Ben, I'd like you to be my liaison with Colonel Black and her staff. I cannot deal with her. I think you have more power to influence her than I do. I don't know any other way to protect David."

"I can do that," Ben said. "So … National Security is involved?" His eyes began to sparkle.

"Yes."

He nodded thoughtfully.

"Thanks for your help, Ben. I knew I could count on you."

Ben walked me to the door. "I'll do what I can, Mrs. McCloud."

It was 3:30 p.m. Time to put my plans for Operation Family into action again. I looked out the sliding glass door into the back yard. The children were playing with Freckles and having a blast. The sun had peeked out from behind the clouds, awakening brilliant colors. Bright green grass, glowing purple asters in a wooden tub, a few golden leaves still clinging to the maple tree, patches of azure in the sky above—all displaying the glory of the late autumn day.

Sliding the door open, I leaned out. "Ryan! Suzanna! It's time for us to go visit Dad."

"Okay," they called in unison.

Ryan scooped Freckles up in his arms and followed Suzanna inside. The children's cheeks glowed, and they smelled of fresh air. The puppy, smelling like damp dog, wiggled and squirmed to get down.

"Put Freckles in the laundry room with his water and food," I said. "Then wash up and change into clean clothes."

I fastened my loose curls with mother-of-pearl barrettes, leaving the rest of my hair to cascade down my back the way David liked it. I grabbed the science and math books from the table.

"Ryan," I called, "bring the games from the kitchen. I'm going to the car."

"Mama, can we bring Freckles?" Suzanna raced down the hall toward me.

"No, honey. He needs to stay here. They don't allow dogs at the hospital."

The door to Ryan's room slammed and he hurried out, grabbed the games, and headed for the car we had rented for our stay in Oklahoma. Together, the three of us headed toward David and our daily family time.

The main lobby was busy, with officers leaving for home and others coming to work. But there were no visitors sitting in the lobby chairs. There never were. While the children moved the magazines aside and arranged our books and games, I went to fetch David from the library.

Now that he was working, he was allowed to wear his uniform during the day. It was a relief to see him regaining some self-respect. But he was thin, and his eyes looked tired.

"Hi, honey." I walked into his embrace.

"Hi, Lissa."

We stood there for a minute in the stacks, savoring this moment alone. "The children are in the lobby." I stepped back and smiled at him.

"Let's go." David took my hand and we walked toward the children.

"Daddy!" Suzanna ran to him and threw her arms around his waist.

A few officers glanced our way, and Ben leaned out of his office and waved.

"Hey, Dad," Ryan said. "I taught Freckles to sit today!"

"Well, kind of," I said.

We sat together on the leather couch. Suzanna snuggled up on David's right while Ryan talked excitedly about the puppy. Soon the books came out. David went over Ryan's math and science lessons, answering questions and making suggestions about homework.

People strode by, moving toward the door or the elevators, sending curious glances at us. But we ignored them. We were in our own little world together. After a time, we brought out the games. We laughed, talked, and shared the events of the day.

When dinnertime rolled around, we headed for the cafeteria and found a table together. We held hands and thanked God for the food and for his blessings, and we took our time eating and talking. Afterward, we played catch on the hospital lawn, a lawn that seldom served any purpose except providing decoration for the hospital. It became our daily playground.

I was concerned about David. He was becoming more and more sedated from the Haldol. His verbal responses were slow and tired. Though he was happy to see us, I could see him struggling to keep up with the conversation. And I noticed his hands were beginning to tremble. Was it from the drugs?

19

HOLDING GROUND

I T WAS THE third week of November, David's second week on Haldol. Every Monday morning he had to report to the psychiatrist for "therapy" sessions. Now that he was on Haldol, he would express feelings of defeat when we would meet each Monday, saying this was all his fault, that the psychiatrists were right.

I sensed he had fallen under the spell of Haldol—and the lies being shoved down his throat by the psychiatrists. I cried out in my prayer time, "God, what should I do?"

A thought came to mind: The psychiatrists were trying to brainwash David through the use of Haldol. But they saw him only once a week. I saw him daily. He was still on Haldol—and he trusted me. I could use the drug's effects to help him! If I reminded him each Monday evening of the true history of this nightmare, reminded him of the illegal activities, reminded him of the congressional support—just maybe he would snap out of it. I needed to tell him the *truth* about the situation. Maybe the truth would set him free.

From that point, every time David expressed defeat, I would remind him of the true circumstances that led up to his confinement in the psychiatric ward. Usually by the time Wednesday rolled around, he was back on track, resisting the psychiatrists.

But I wondered how much of this he could stand. It was a huge gamble. Yet it seemed my only way to combat the brainwashing.

The weekend of Thanksgiving, the psychiatrists finally agreed to let David come home after work each day and on weekends. That was a time of rejoicing. Things would seem more normal. I could tell from watching the children that they were happier.

But behind the scenes in the early afternoons, my battle to free David continued. Could I get him out of the army intact? These thoughts stayed with me as I prepared our dinner on Thanksgiving day and helped the children with their contributions. Yet the festive preparations distracted me enough to lighten my spirits.

Ryan liked to make the pumpkin pie, so his part of the day came first. He needed little help as he rolled out the pie crust and mixed the filling. With a satisfied smile, he slid the pie into the oven and set the timer.

"My turn! My turn!" Suzanna said.

"Okay, sweetie, you get the chocolate chips and I'll get the oatmeal." I cleared the table for the next round of baking. Suzanna always made the cookies.

David stuck his head in the kitchen and grinned. "Any bowls for me to lick yet?"

"Not unless you like raw pumpkin."

"No thanks!"

"Daddy, I'll have cookies soon," Suzanna said. "You can lick that bowl. Okay?"

"Sure, honey." David sat down next to her, swiping a chocolate chip from the pile.

Suzanna grinned and moved a generous pile toward her dad. "You can have these, too, Daddy. But no more! The rest have to go in the cookies."

"Thanks, honey." David smiled back and popped another chocolate chip into his mouth.

The delicious smells in the kitchen grew by the hour. When we finally sat down to eat, the table was laden with roast turkey, cranberries, mashed potatoes, gravy, green beans, and other dishes. On the counter, cookies and pie waited. We gathered around the dinner table and gave thanks to the Lord for bringing us all together and making this truly a day of thanksgiving.

It was wonderful having David home again. For the first time in months, my heart relaxed enough to feel the Lord's presence among us. It was very good.

I had not exhausted the list Colonel Duffy had given me. After Thanksgiving weekend, I contacted Colonel Stapleton, the psychiatrist who had been at Owen Army Hospital when we first arrived. He had been replaced by Colonel Kant a few months later.

"Colonel Stapleton, this is Lissa McCloud, David McCloud's wife."

"Yes! Lissa! It's good to hear from you. How are you all doing?"

"Not good at all, sir. Colonels Aiken and Barnett tried to involve David in illegal activities. When David wouldn't go along, they had him committed involuntarily to Spires Army Medical Center's psychiatric ward."

"What! I can't believe it! David is a great radiologist, and I felt he had always been a well-balanced person. This is unreal!"

"Colonel, could you write a letter to the IG here to that effect? We need some help."

There was silence. Finally he said, "No, I can't. My word carries weight as a psychiatrist, and I haven't examined David."

"But Colonel, all I'm asking is for you to relate your initial impressions of David."

"Lissa, I can't get involved. Our job as psychiatrists in the military is to mediate between the command and the staff and to keep things running smoothly."

"Colonel, we're looking for *truth* and *justice* here!"

His voice became venomous. "Forget about justice, Lissa! You won't find it in the military. You very seldom find it in real life. The only place you'll find justice is when you're a little kid and you can run to mama and she fixes it!" He paused, then changed his tone, trying to be persuasive. "Lissa, don't think of this as something bad. Think of it as David isn't compatible with the army, and this is their way of firing him. It's not so bad!"

"That would be fine if it didn't affect his credentials as a doctor and his entire work future!"

"Well," he said, "If it were *my* credentials, I guess I would fight, too. But let's face it: the military is a gang of men that runs around murdering people. Sure, they wave little flags in front of them to justify it, but the fact is, they're a bunch of thugs. What they're doing to David isn't going to cause them a twinge of conscience. Maybe something like My Lai[11] would, but not this."

I listened in shock and finally managed to close the conversation. This was coming from a *military psychiatrist!* But then, he had been the one who had put Dr. Olsen and Dr. Peters into psychiatric treatment against their will, on orders from Colonel Barnett. He was no better than the men who were trying to destroy David. He was part of the corrupt system.

Why had I expected him to be honorable? I sat rubbing my forehead, where a headache was beginning to throb.

This was an emotional roller coaster.

It was now coming up on December. It had been nearly six months since David first told me about the problems he faced at Owen Army Hospital. Six months of agonizing. Six months of prayer ... yet David's situation did not improve. Instead, he was slowly disintegrating, falling deeper into the morass of hopelessness—a victim of the political battle raging between the Army Medical Corps and Congress.

Spiritually, I was barely coping. My prayers were simple: "Lord, help us! Help us! Save David, your servant!" I was in spiritual shock. God had not intervened, and I had nothing else to say. God was silent. Yes, I knew he was with us, but I felt no comfort—for the first time in my life. I had to depend on the prayers of others on our behalf.

My spiritual mom and David's mother had organized prayer teams. A handful of close friends had done the same. Each week I called the prayer teams, updating them and giving specific requests. Then, after speaking with them, I moved on with the work at hand—emotionally stunned but going through the motions regardless of my feelings.

I was finally able to connect with Lt. Colonel Ingermann, the former chief of resource management at Owen Army Hospital. I had met him only once when we were in the Philippines. He struck me as being all business.

"Yes, Lissa. I remember David," he said. "I had to have some X-rays for a broken wrist, and he spoke with me. I met him on a few occasions in the officers' mess, too."

"Colonel Ingermann, David was told to alter some time cards and to do some other illegal things, but he refused. Now his commanding officers have put him in the psychiatric ward at Spires AMC in retaliation. Can you tell me what you know about the illegal practices at Owen Army Hospital?"

Colonel Ingermann swore. "It's just like those men to do this! Yes, I know all about the shenanigans going on there. Colonel Barnett approached me the first year I was there. I wasn't even under his command. I reported to Colonel Calloway. But Colonel Barnett asked me to allow the time card situation because he said they needed to pay those who had worked under the old system—before Congress passed the law about no waste, fraud, or abuse and spelled out the laws. He said he was in the process of phasing out the practice. He also said my officer's evaluation report [OER] would reflect my cooperation ... or lack of it. He said if I allowed this practice, he would square it with Colonel Calloway and make sure I received a good OER. If I didn't allow it, I'd be in trouble. Lissa, you know how a bad OER can end a career!" He begged me to understand.

"I went along with it the first year, thinking the commanders would clean up their act and stop the fraud. But by end of the year, I could see they weren't going to do it. Colonel Barnett had been lying to me! Then Colonel Calloway gave me a blistering OER, setting me back years in my career. Colonel Barnett had not come through with his support. So I called the IG and reported them. I knew Colonel Aiken and Colonel Barnett would retaliate, so I arranged with Colonel Duffy to transfer to his command before I blew the whistle. That way they couldn't touch me."

"Can you put this in writing?"

"Uh—no. My report on the fraud is in an IG report in Hawaii. I can't risk writing this testimony, Lissa. But I *can* send you a copy of a previous IG report. It's been floating around Washington, D.C. for about a year. A friend has a copy. He used it to defend himself against retaliation, too. I'm sure it will help you."

"That would be wonderful, Colonel Ingermann!"

"I'll have it in the mail tomorrow."

"Thank you so much!" I had tried to get an IG report from Pacific Command in Hawaii, but they had refused to send it, stating I had no need for it. The new Freedom of Information Act was not honored.

"Lissa, keep in touch with me and let me know how this goes," Colonel Ingermann said. "I'll do whatever I can behind the scenes. I'm sorry David got caught in this mess."

"I really appreciate this, Colonel. I'll take you up on your offer." I breathed a sigh of relief. Surely the IG report would help free David.

When the report arrived, I read it through. Many pages contained handwritten testimony. Some of that testimony was incredibly brave. The report documented the waste, fraud, and abuse at Owen Army Hospital—and the pressure the commander was putting on all the officers and staff. This document was gold!

But since the Spires hospital commanders were arrayed against Congress, participating in the corruption by ignoring it, I knew it would do no good to show *them* the report. The time would come, however, when this testimony would help us somehow. I made a copy for Mr. Goodman, then put the report in my arsenal of testimony and waited for the time to use it.

20

THE PRESIDENT
(DECEMBER)

THE NEXT MORNING, I made a chart of all the people in the command structure, for I was trying to follow the army's chain of command. I checked off all the people I had already contacted. At that point, twenty senior officers, including four generals and an admiral, were involved in the case in some way. Yet no one had intervened to save David. The only person I knew to contact next was the president of the United States, the commander-in-chief of the armed forces.

I wasn't sure if he would help, but I had to ask.

After breakfast, the children and I cleared the table and got out the schoolbooks.

"Children, we are going to do something different today. We are going to write to the president of the United States and ask *him* to get Dad out of this situation. Are you with me?"

Both children nodded, their eyes wide with wonder.

"First, you should write this: Dear Mr. President ..."

When the letters were finished, here is what they wrote:

Dear Mr. President,

My dad told about illegal things that were happening in the Philippines where he was working. His commander had him put in a psychiatric ward. There are a lot of important men who saw what happened, and they have been trying to get him out. But nobody seems to be able to do it. It's like they are watching a bear chewing up on Dad, and they're all standing around wringing their hands, wondering what to do. Nobody has the brains to shoot the bear!

Mr. President, will you "shoot the bear" and get my dad out of this, please?

Sincerely,
Ryan McCloud

THE PRESIDENT

Dear Mr. President,
    Please make the bad guys let my Daddy go!
                        Suzanna

I wrote a cover letter, telling what had happened to David. Together, we prayed over the letters, put them in an envelope, and mailed them to the president.

We never heard from him. But we learned that he ordered the Department of the Army inspector general to conduct an investigation. I heard about it from my DAIG contact. He was ticked. Though the DAIG was already investigating, the president's order made the investigation far more demanding. Now they would have to report to the highest authority in the land with their investigation.

But all this did was to step up the pressure on David, for the psychiatrists feared for their jobs and their own freedom. If they were found guilty of complicity in this crime, they would face court-martial. They were in too far to back out. They had to win or go down. If ever there was a time for the commanding general of Spires to stop what was happening to David and save his own skin, it was now.

But he did not.

By mid December, I had pounded on every door in the military chain of command structure. Looking at my list, I had crossed off every name that might help. Yet nothing had changed. What should I do now? Take it to the press? I had tried involving the press, but no agency was interested in the story. The army had labeled David "delusional." Who would believe us under those circumstances?

How about a petition? Could anything be achieved that way? Maybe. The one thing the military feared was bad publicity, for it meant that congressmen and senators might cut off their flow of money.

To whom should I address the petition? Hmmm. Yes. The surgeon general of the army. I called Lewis and Ruth to discuss the possibilities.

"We have prayer groups in seven states that are praying for us," I said. "If we send petitions to them, maybe we can gather enough signatures to alarm the surgeon general."

"Yes," Ruth said. "I think we can get a lot out here in California."

"I think we should do it," Lewis said.

"Get it ready," Ruth said, "but let's wait until after Christmas. People are preoccupied with their own families right now."

"Okay. I'll put it together and send you a copy. Then as soon as New Year's is done, we'll get it moving."

Afterward, I sat down at the computer and composed the petition:

To the Surgeon General of the Army:

We, the undersigned, have been told of all that has been done to Major David McCloud, M.D., former Chief of Radiology at Owen Army Hospital in the Philippines. We are aware that Colonels Aiken and Barnett asked him to sign time cards that were in violation of Army law, and to provide services to ineligible civilians, also illegally. We are aware that those commanders used the Army psychiatrists to falsely accuse Major McCloud of having delusions after he refused to do what they requested and had reported the above activities to the Department of the Army inspector general. We know of the anti-retaliatory law that forbids the command from sending anyone for psychiatric evaluation after he has "blown the whistle." We believe Major McCloud's civil rights have been grossly violated and we petition you to *stop this at once*. We want Major McCloud's name cleared, his medical files erased of the false diagnosis, and proper restoration of Major McCloud to his position as a radiologist. Please do not allow this disgrace to our nation to continue!

That should do it, I thought. I sent a copy to Lewis and Ruth, and waited for the new year.

Winter snows were falling. They felt bitterly cold after our year in the Philippines. The children adapted more easily than David and I. The children built snow forts and snowmen and had snowball fights, filling the air with laughter.

Every week, I called everyone on my list who was in a position to help free David. I was determined to be the "squeaky wheel," to never let them rest until they had freed my husband from this unjust situation. By limiting myself to one call a day, I was able to manage the emotional struggle. I found it hard to badger people! It drained me, physically and emotionally. But it had to be done.

Living in a neighborhood again and having other homemakers around was a blessing. I became better acquainted with them, getting together for tea or coffee and talking about our families. It took some time before I opened up about our situation. It was important that the children have a place to play where their friends would accept them, so I was slow to trust others with the information.

Dawn, my neighbor across the street, listened to the story without surprise. "I've heard of what Spires does to people in their psychiatric ward," she said. "You aren't the first with this story."

"You *know* about this?"

"Yes. It's the standard way the army handles whistleblowers. If anyone rocks the boat, his commanding officer puts him in the psych ward and has him declared delusional. David isn't the first."

"Oh!"

"Listen," Dawn said. "You need to get your husband to a psychiatrist in the city. Have him talk with your husband. David seems just fine to me, and I think the psychiatrist will say the same thing. It would be another way to get around those creeps at Spires."

After our chat, I looked up psychiatrists in the yellow pages. I called a Dr. Brewer, whose ad looked good, and made an appointment for David for after work on the first Friday in January. It was all I could do before Christmas. Now it was time for concentrating on our family and celebrating Jesus' birth.

Whenever I think of Christmas in Oklahoma, I remember the cheerful lights gleaming from the houses that lined the road to our pastor's house. We were headed for a Christmas party. His windows, trees, and walkway were lined with beautiful lights, and the delightful smell of ginger cookies and hot apple cider greeted us as he opened the door.

Pastor John welcomed us to his home. I joined the women in the kitchen while the children found their friends and David joined the men around the fireplace, keeping his hands in his pockets to hide the trembling caused by Haldol.

I remember feeling engulfed by comfort ... cheerful words ... and deep, Christian love from those who gathered. I don't remember details. Just feelings.

I remember our children laughing and playing with the other children. I remember the clink of glass as Pastor John's wife served the punch. I remember sinking into a comfortable chair and breathing in the atmosphere of peace.

Sometimes simple gifts of hospitality and love can overcome all despair. That night, I was able to look beyond our nightmare and feel ... really feel ... the love of Christ toward us. I have savored the memory of that night through the years.

Yes, the family of God reached into our pain and gently wrapped their arms around our bruised souls. Our Christian brothers and sisters gave us respite. They gave us strength. We were new to this group, yet they loved us for Jesus. They had healing hands and kind, generous hearts.

It was an island of peace and rest in the midst of the swamp of pain and exhaustion.

What I did not know was that one of the other guests was a JAG officer from Fort Hardin. Pastor John had told him about our circumstances and the attorney was watching us, weighing the story in his mind, listening to our conversation. God had placed him there for this moment, to help us. But that evening, we knew nothing of his background. We simply soaked up the warmth and let the body of Christ minister to us.

21

UNEXPECTED ALLIES
(JANUARY)

David's narrative:

I can't believe it's already January—and the army inspector general has not even begun investigating my report. I feel caught in limbo. The Haldol the psychiatrist gave me is making my body shake. First, it was just a tremor in my hands. Now it's affecting my feet, too. It's embarrassing. And I can't think clearly with this drug in my system. Everything seems remote, like I'm in a different world. Dad did some research on Haldol and said this drug-induced palsy can become permanent. That's one of the side effects. Lissa and I talked it over, and I've decided to stop taking it.

This week I discovered that Lissa has been fighting to get me out of this mess, though I asked her not to. I should have suspected something was up when she seemed so submissive in agreeing to stay out of it. She is fearless! How can I protect her if she insists on helping me? I am afraid for her! These people are utterly ruthless! I will have to start overseeing what she does. Maybe I can stand between her and danger that way.

NEW YEAR'S DAY passed. It was time to mail the petition to our friends. I called people around the country and asked for their help. Most were willing. Some held back because of their positions in the military. Some feared they would suffer for helping David. But a great number of friends were eager to sign and circulate the petition.

David felt much better in January. His headaches finally disappeared, along with the fever, and his skin was no longer yellow. Whatever illness had been plaguing him seemed to be gone.

The interview with Dr. Brewer, the civilian psychiatrist, went well. By then, David had pulled out of the Haldol side effects. He was clear and concise, and his hands no longer shook. Dr. Brewer met with David three times to confirm his findings, then wrote a letter for us to help free David from Spires AMC. It was a long, detailed report, but the main thrust was this:

> I would like for it to be clearly heard that I think what is happening to Dr. David McCloud is an absurd outrage to the profession of medicine and to the creditability of the United States Army.
>
> I am urging you to evaluate Dr. McCloud from the standpoint of his abilities and what he can do for the U.S. Army. If you cannot do this, I feel that you are playing a crucial role in disgracing this man for the rest of his professional career. In my opinion, Dr. McCloud showed true patriotism by standing up for what is right for both the United States Army and the United States of America. If he is forced to go before the Medical Review Board for these trumped up, false accusations, this could become a landmark case …
>
> After evaluating Dr. McCloud, speaking with his wife, and reviewing information from the aforementioned source, it is my opinion that Dr. McCloud does not suffer from a psychiatric disorder.
>
> Colonel (Ret.) Mel Brewer, M.D.

I sent copies of the letter to Colonel Erickson (to be given to Admiral Grady), to our congressman and senator, to the Department of the Army inspector general, to the Spires AMC command, and to Major Ben Duggan.

The Spires psychiatrists were furious! Ben, with a smile, told me about their anger at my going to an outside psychiatrist for an opinion. By now, he was firmly on our side, and we were on a first-name basis.

But the pressure was growing. I was not used to political maneuvering. My simple, uncomplicated life had become intense, and I tired easily. Even at night I could not escape the pressures of the day.

But one night, early in January, I had a vivid dream. I was standing inside a log home looking out a large picture window. There were two such windows. A rustic deck wrapped around the house, overlooking a slope clad with young pine trees. Above me rose a cathedral ceiling. I turned. Behind me a staircase led to a balcony, a loft bedroom. A gentle breeze blew against my cheeks from an open door, and I heard the sounds of a small creek. I felt so at peace!

Then I awoke. The room was dark, with a faint hint of moonlight at the window. I rose on my elbow and leaned toward my sleeping husband. "David! David!" I whispered, shaking him gently.

"Mph. Huh?"

"David! I just had the best dream!"

"Mmmm."

"Let me tell you ..."

His eyes opened, and he watched my face as I described it to him.

"Oh, David. If only I could be in that house!"

"Uh-huh."

I slipped my hand into his, put my head on his shoulder, and sighed. We drifted back to sleep, and I was comforted by the dream. The peace stayed with me long into the next day. Someday, I thought—I knew—we will live in that house. Someday, there will be peace.

The second week in January, a reporter called. I had tried to get the attention of the news media to help us, but without any success. Now a reporter I'd never contacted was calling me.

"My name is Jill Maynard, with Shoreline News & National Commentary. Yesterday, a detective who often gives us tips told me about your situation with the army. He said his granddaughter went to school with your son before you went to the Philippines." She mentioned the name of the family, and I recognized them at once. They were good friends.

Wow!

"Our source tells me your story is credible and that you are reliable. I would be interested in it, if you are willing to share."

"Oh, yes!" Finally. The power of the press is incredible. Many call it the fourth branch of government, and the military fears it like nothing else. This was very good news.

I briefed Jill on the facts of the case and agreed to send her a summary with documentation. Elation filled my heart!

"Thank you, Mrs. McCloud. I will look forward to reading what you have, and I will start researching this. You do understand that we must be very careful to have all the facts before printing a piece like this about the military?"

"I do understand. And please call me Lissa."

"Okay, Lissa. Let's keep in touch. Here's my phone number ..."

After replacing the phone, I danced around the room, clapping and swinging Suzanna up from her chair to join me. Ryan came into the room, and I pulled him into the circle. The children laughed and begged to know what was happening.

"The newspapers are going to help Daddy!"

"Whoa!" Ryan shouted.

"Yay!" Suzanna squealed.

What an emotional boost! I was flying high when David came home that night. When I told him about our newspaper contact, he smiled broadly. Surely the tide was shifting.

Later that week, our lawyer, Mr. Goodman, called. "Mrs. McCloud, you're not going to believe this. There is a woman sitting here in my office telling me a story just like yours. Would you be willing to talk with her?"

"Yes!" I said.

"Her name is Nancy Haven. She's a sergeant."

I spoke with Nancy briefly and invited her to our home to talk. She came right over.

She was a tall woman, several years older than I was, and she was wearing fatigues. She had short, brown hair and sad, brown eyes. Over tea and cookies, Nancy told me her story.

"My husband, Jerry, was a sergeant working as a mechanic in Korea. He has been in the army since he was a kid, and he's close to retirement. His boss was making him and the other mechanics use old, broken, and rusted replacement parts for the vehicles they were repairing. About half the vehicles would break down later … in the field. He told his colonel about it, and his colonel told him to shut up. But he didn't. So the colonel made Jerry do paperwork in a storage closet with a guard at the door.

"After three months, the colonel told Jerry that he appeared to be depressed—and had him shipped here to Spires! Now he is confined to the psychiatric ward under the care of Captain Carver, who said Jerry is suffering from mental illness. Jerry said they are treating him really bad—that those people are not there to help him."

Nancy's eyes brimmed with tears. "We've been married only two years. It's not fair!"

"I know what you mean," I said. "There is something very wrong going on here." I handed her a box of tissues. "What are you doing to get him out?"

"I've talked with the *Stars & Stripes*, the military newspaper. They're planning to run a story on what's happening."

"Good! The press is our best friend right now." I told her about David and our own battle.

"That's just like what they're doing to Jerry!"

"Have you talked with your congressman or senator yet?"

"Yes. We're from California, and I've called their offices about this."

"From California! So are we!"

Nancy stared at me for a moment. "Are you a Christian?"

"Yes!"

"So are we!"

Our men were from the same state, with the same senator, with the same faith, facing the same situation under the same psychiatrist, with the same harsh treatment … and now, the same lawyer. There was no way this was a coincidence. It was a God-thing.

Two identical cases would give us both more credibility with the press. "Let's keep in touch," I said.

"Yes!" Nancy's eyes looked more hopeful now.

"Maybe we can help each other." We exchanged phone numbers.

I walked her to her car and asked the Lord to bless her. My heart lifted to God in praise, for clearly he had brought us together to help each other in this battle.

22

THE BATTLE EXPANDS

David's narrative:

Last week, Lissa told me about another man who is going through the same thing I am. Today Jerry Haven came down to the hospital library where I work, and we talked some. He said he asked Dr. Carver about me, and Dr. Carver forbade Jerry to talk with me. He came here anyway. Though I am sad to see him suffering, too, it's a great comfort to have another brother in Christ walking through this with me.

A WINTER STORM swept through Oklahoma, depositing four inches of snow. Snowplows roared through town, clearing the roads. The neighborhood children, at home with schools closed for the day, built snowmen and snow forts. I left Suzanna and Ryan with my neighbor, Dawn, and drove to Spires.

After stomping the snow off my boots, I crossed the lobby to Major Ben Duggan's office. His door stood open.

"Hi, Ben," I called.

"Hi, Lissa! Come on in." He waved me to a chair.

"Did the Haven situation check out?"

"Yes. I looked it up, and his claims are just like David's." He looked curiously at me. "How did his wife end up at your lawyer's office?"

I laughed. "It's a God-thing, Ben."

"I see." Ben shook his head and smiled. "The Department of the Army inspector general will be here on Friday. She will want to speak with you and with David."

Finally! It has been many months since David asked for their help, and the IG has done nothing to stop the retaliation. But I guess it's better late than never, I thought.

"What's the DAIG like?"

"This one is a woman. Her name is Ms. Williams. She's about fifteen or twenty years older than you, I guess."

"All right." I nodded.

"So I'll see you here at ten o'clock Friday morning?"

"You bet." I smiled and stood to leave. "Ben, thanks for all your help."

"That's what I'm here for."

Friday came quickly. During that week I organized all the testimony and put together an affidavit to give to the DAIG ... with the exception of the IG report Colonel Ingermann had given me. My having that report might anger the DAIG and hurt David. It seemed better to use it with the JAG. Even without that report, I had plenty of proof of the situation.

Standing in front of the mirror, I checked my appearance: trim red skirt, white blouse, red heels, red and gold earrings. My hair hung loose on my shoulders, long and smooth. Taking a deep breath, I left for the interview, hopeful that my testimony would help David out of this situation.

The snow had melted and the sun was peeking through the clouds as I drove up to Spires. The DAIG was talking with Ben when I entered the outer office. She was tall, thin, and wearing a severe black dress, with just a tiny strip of white edging at the high neckline.

"Mrs. McCloud," Ben said, motioning me into his office. "This is the Department of the Army inspector general, Ms. Williams."

"Hello." I nodded.

"Hello, Mrs. McCloud," she said. "Won't you be seated?"

For the next hour, Ms. Williams grilled me about the situation.

"When did this all begin? What did your husband say? What did other people say? Who was involved?" Methodically and with a detached air, she listened to my account. Wherever possible, I backed up my report with written testimony from others. I gave her copies of the letters from Colonel Calloway, Major Ralston, and Colonel Leigh, and a copy of the outside psychiatrist's report. I handed her the affidavit testifying to everything others had told me about the situation. I told her about Admiral Grady's involvement in trying to free David. I gave her copies of every bit of written evidence in my possession—except for the IG report from Colonel Ingermann, which she already had—in hopes it would show her the truth about David.

All the while, Ben sat behind his desk and listened, a witness to the conversation.

When we were finished, she stood and said, "Thank you for your testimony, Mrs. McCloud." She ushered me out the door into the outer office, where David now waited. "Major McCloud, please come in."

David touched my hand as our paths crossed.

Feeling nervous, I waited in the outer office and prayed.

David's testimony was much shorter. He was a headline communicator and far more concise than I. When he finished, he came out with a cautious smile. I knew he felt good about the interview.

Ms. Williams stepped out of Ben's office. "I appreciate your speaking with me today. I will take this information back and process it. When we have made a determination, I will send you a report." She stepped back into Ben's office and closed the door.

David's arms encircled me, and we just stood there for a moment. Now all we could do was wait. Surely the truth would come out.

Ms. Williams's next stop would be the Philippines. It was supposed to be a secret inspection. Nobody was supposed to know when she would arrive—a plan designed to catch people unprepared. We hoped her visit would shed some light on the corruption there, that she would find testimony about what had really happened.

So we waited and prayed.

The night was pitch black. It was less than a week since we had spoken to Ms. Williams. I had been sound asleep when something jerked me awake. The air was filled with fear, and I felt an evil presence in the room. David moaned. His head tossed back and forth on his pillow.

I sat up, chilled with terror. My eyes searched the dark, conscious of something far beyond my spiritual experience. There was a demonic presence in the room. I threw back the covers and fled to the hallway, terrified at the presence of such great evil.

"Jesus!" I whispered. "Help us! Protect us!"

Ryan cried out in his sleep. I went into his room and knelt beside him, placing my hands over him. "Jesus! Protect my child! Protect my children!"

Suzanna began crying. I ran to her room, stretched my arms over her, and cried out softly, "Jesus! Help us!"

But the evil presence would not leave.

For the next hour, I prayed over my children as they cried out in their sleep. But I could not go into the room where David lay, tossing and turning, moaning. I could only stand at the doorway, holding my hands out toward him, calling on the name of Jesus to protect my husband.

Toward the end of the hour, I huddled, cold and shivering, on the couch in the living room and prayed over and over, "The Lord is my shepherd! The Lord is my shepherd!" Finally, the evil presence left. I crept back into bed, wrapped my arms around David, and prayed for his protection until I eventually fell asleep.

I did not wish to frighten David or the children by telling them what had happened during the night. But the next day, I called my spiritual dad and told him. "Dad, a demon was in our house last night! My friends in the Philippines warned me that some of the Filipino doctors were practicing witchcraft and voodoo against us. I think they are doing it again, probably because of the coming investigation. What should I do?"

"Lissa, you must pray against the demon in the name of Jesus. Spend your day praising Jesus and calling on his name."

He prayed for me over the phone. "Our gracious heavenly Father, I ask that you will fill Lissa's house with your presence. Do not let the forces of Satan touch this family!"

As the words of his prayer poured over me, peace fell on my heart. I could picture Dad's kind eyes and gentle smile, this man of God who had taught me so much about living for Jesus.

I also called a dear friend on the West Coast who had experienced similar demonic activity. She told me to sing praise songs to Jesus all day, and to pray at every window and door that the blood of Jesus would shield us from the enemy.

That was good advice. During the day, I sang praises to Jesus frequently, and I prayed for the blood of Jesus to cover us. By evening, a great peace had settled on my spirit.

David and I prayed with the children as usual and went to bed.

Again, in the dead of night, I awoke. Again, I felt the presence of evil in our room. But this time I placed my hands over David and spoke into the darkness, "This man is covered by the blood of Jesus. This house and this family are under the blood of Jesus. We are under his protection. You have no authority here. In Jesus' name, leave!"

For the next fifteen minutes, I battled the evil spirit. Finally, defeated by the power of Jesus' name, it left.

I settled down into the warm blankets and fell asleep, peace flooding my soul.

The demon never returned.

Snowstorms swept across Oklahoma as January drew to a close. Bitter cold held the town in its grip. Yet in the midst of the storms, the petitions began filtering in, warm affirmations of support from friends and acquaintances across the nation. When the petitions were all in my hands, I called David's parents.

"Mom! Dad! We have 525 signatures on the petitions!"

"Good!" Ruth said.

"That should be enough to get the surgeon general's attention," Lewis said. "When are you sending them in?"

"I'm going to write a cover letter to go with them, and I'll make copies for our records. I'll have the petition in the mail this afternoon."

Ryan stood at the table, looking at the stack of signed petitions. Then he looked up at me, his eyes glowing. "A lot of people are trying to help Dad, aren't they?"

"Yes." I smiled and hugged him.

He gave a deep sigh. His heart was so bruised by what was happening to his father. This petition and all those signatures gave him hope.

Taking the children with me, I drove to Kinko's and photocopied the petition. The staff at Kinko's knew all about the case. I'd been there at least once a week since November, making copies or sending faxes to various officials. They gathered around me, asking about the petition and how it went, exchanging smiles and congratulating me on the number of signatures.

I placed the original petition and the cover letter in an envelope addressed to the surgeon general of the army and left, waving to my friends at Kinko's. Ryan and Suzanna waved, too, flashing bright smiles. Together we went to the post office and mailed the envelope. Now we would wait. Again.

But first we celebrated. We went to a local restaurant and ordered hot fudge sundaes. Our hearts were filled with encouragement at the show of support from friends across the nation. We were blessed.

That night, I showed David a copy of the petition—covered with signatures of friends and people we didn't even know who wanted to help.

His eyes glowed. "Wow!" His shoulders straightened, and a smile spread across his face. There was hope in his eyes.

23

THE THICK OF BATTLE
(FEBRUARY)

I T WAS SUNDAY afternoon, the first weekend of February. The snow had melted. Pale dried grass, naked oak and elm trees, and rivulets of water surrounded our house as we sat down to lunch.

We had just finished eating when the phone rang.

"Lissa, this is Brad Ingermann."

"Hi, Colonel Ingermann."

David tensed and turned to face me. Suzanna and Ryan had already left the table to play with the puppy.

"I just got a call from a friend in the Philippines. He said that Colonel Barnett and the Owen Hospital staff know all about the coming DAIG's visit. It's set for February 5. Colonel Barnett has all his allies lined up to testify. Someone in the travel office leaked the information to him."

A chill went up my spine.

"I thought you should know."

"Thank you, Colonel Ingermann." I felt frozen inside.

"What did he say?" David walked over to me.

I didn't want to tell him.

"What is it?"

I sighed. "Colonel Barnett knows the date of the DAIG's visit."

David's face went pale. "Colonel Barnett has set me up!" He wandered into the living room and collapsed onto the couch. His eyes were glazed. "They are going to destroy me!"

All hope had left him. This was the straw that broke David.

I sat next to him and put my arms around him. He was tense, unyielding. "David? Can you talk about it?"

He could not. He was terrified. Hunched over on the couch, he did not move for more than an hour. I could not reach him.

"Daddy?" Suzanna slipped up on the couch beside him and stroked his arm.

But David did not respond.

Ryan sat in a chair across the room, frozen with helplessness, watching his dad, not sure what to do.

Finally, I put a call through to the civilian psychiatrist who had helped us. His answering machine was on, so I left a message. By that evening, we were sitting in his office. David was still in a state of terror.

"Dr. Brewer, I don't know what to do! I've never seen David like this!"

"You must not let him go to work at Spires tomorrow!" the doctor said. "Those psychiatrists must not be allowed to see him like this! I will give him some medicine to stabilize him. It will take a few days to start working. But have him call in sick until it kicks in."

"Okay," I said, tears in my eyes.

I helped David out to the car and drove home. Ryan and Suzanna met us at the door.

"How's Dad?" Ryan asked.

"He isn't well," I said. "But Dr. Brewer gave him some medicine. He said Dad shouldn't go to work tomorrow."

Suzanna wrapped her arms around David. "It's okay, Daddy. It's okay."

But David didn't respond.

I helped him into the bedroom, where he lay on the bed and stared at the ceiling. I unlaced his shoes and began to undress him. As I pulled the blanket over his unresponsive form, I whispered, "David, it will be all right."

I slid to my knees and silently cried out to God for David. Hearing sobs outside our bedroom door, I arose and went to comfort Ryan and Suzanna, who were sitting together on the carpet outside our room, crying for their father. I sank to my knees, wrapped my arms around them, and just held them.

It was a very long night. After I finally persuaded the children to go to bed, I went back into our bedroom and slid into bed with David, cradling him in my arms and praying softly for him as he slept, crying out to God to restore him.

The next morning, David was still in a trance-like state. Silently, he sat at the table, waiting for breakfast. Ryan slipped into his seat, glancing first at his dad and then at me. Suzanna watched David steadily, her eyes huge, her usual chatter missing.

"David, Dr. Brewer told you to call in sick today." I sat next to him and laid my hand on his arm.

"I have to go in!" David said, his eyes wide and unfocused. Those were his first words all morning.

"No, David. You must stay home today!"

"I have to go in!"

"David! Listen to me!"

But he stood and headed toward the door. "I have to go in!"

I dashed between David and the door. "Stop! David!" I put my hands on his chest and looked up into his eyes. They were blank and unfocused. "David. Look at me!"

But he didn't.

I reached up and slapped his cheek, trying to shock him out of his daze, then stood aghast at what I had done.

He looked at me, his eyes wild and dilated, then walked around me, still in a trance. Ryan stood in front of the door, blocking the exit. "Dad. Don't leave!"

"Daddy!" Suzanna cried out. "Don't go!"

David took Ryan by the shoulders and patiently moved him away.

"No, David!" I cried, grabbing his arm.

"I have to go to work," he said, shaking me off and walking out the door.

Suzanna dropped to the floor, sobbing hysterically.

My legs seemed to give out, and I sank beside her, crying, holding my little girl, trying to comfort her.

Ryan rushed out after David and threw himself in front of the truck's door. "Dad! Don't go! Don't go!"

But David moved him aside, climbed into the truck, and started the engine, still in that trance-like state.

Ryan draped himself over the hood of the truck, trying to keep it from moving. But David inexorably backed it onto the road, slipping away from Ryan's frantic hands and cries.

Ryan walked back into the house past Suzanna and me, went into his room, and shut the door.

Our family was devastated. There was nowhere to turn. David was now fully under the spell of the Spires psychiatrists. He was finally broken.

It was one month after he had stopped taking Haldol.

Yet that afternoon, when the mail arrived, I opened a card from a dear friend. Through tears I read what was printed across the front of the card:

For I know the plans I have for you, declares the Lord, plans to prosper you and not to harm you, plans to give you hope and a future.
—Jeremiah 29:11

God had not forgotten us.

David called from Spires AMC later that day. He had been admitted to the psychiatric ward, and the psychiatrists had made him sign a statement that he wanted to be there. But he felt coerced into signing it. He did not want to be there at all. He wanted to come home.

The psychiatrists would not let me see David that day. He was totally in their power.

The next morning, David called, his voice tight with anxiety. "Lissa, the doctors are saying they want to use electric shock on me. Don't let them!"

"Okay, honey. Hold on! I'll write up a statement saying you felt coerced into signing that you wanted to be on the psychiatric ward, and that you want to go home. You can sign it when I get there."

"Okay."

"I'm coming, David."

The children had eaten their lunch. I asked Ryan to keep an eye on Suzanna and left the two children playing with the puppy.

At Spires, I went straight to the psychiatric ward and found David. He read through the statement and signed it. He wanted to be free! I took the statement to Ben Duggan's office and told him what had happened.

"Ben, the psychiatrists finally broke David. Now they want to use electric shock on him! But we want him to be treated by our own doctor off post, someone we can trust. And he wants to be free to come home at night. He does not want to have to stay here. Can you help me?"

"I am sorry about what has happened to your husband, Lissa. Let me make a copy of David's statement for my own records, then I'll take it up to the ward. Would you like a cup of coffee while I'm gone?"

Ben disappeared for a few minutes, returning with coffee, a newspaper, and a copy of David's statement. "Here, Lissa. I'll be back as soon as possible. Hang in there."

It was twenty minutes before Ben returned. He wasn't happy. "Lissa, the psychiatrists won't let David come home at nights, and yes, they are planning to do electric shock on him."

"No!" Tears welled in my eyes. "They can't! It's torture!"

Ben looked defeated. "I don't know what else to do, Lissa. I have no authority to free him … all I can do is investigate."

I wiped away the tears and reached for the statement. "I'm going to take this to Colonel Austin's office and see if I can get him to order David's release." I headed toward the door.

Moments later, I walked into the office of the deputy commander of clinical services. "Colonel Austin, the psychiatrists have put David back on the ward and refuse to let him come home. They coerced him into signing that he wanted to be there. They are planning to do electric shock on him. Here is David's statement saying he does *not* want to be on the ward, and he does *not* want electric shock treatment. I would like you to order his release."

Colonel Austin, with arrogance written all over his face, said, "No, Mrs. McCloud. I will not release your husband. That is final."

I walked out of his office.

Returning to Ben's office briefly, I told him of Colonel Austin's refusal to release David. "Thank you for trying to help, Ben. I've got some phone calls to make now."

"Good luck, Lissa." Ben sighed, defeat written in his eyes.

Back at the house, I called Paul Gambol at National Security and told him what had happened. "Paul, the doctors at Spires AMC are going to use electric shock on David. I want him out of there! We have a civilian doctor we trust, and I want my husband to be able to use his services. Those psychiatrists at Spires mean him harm!"

"Lissa, let me make a phone call. I will get him out!"

"Thank you, Paul."

I sat at the table with the children, too emotionally exhausted to concentrate.

"Are the bad people going to let Daddy go?" Suzanna asked.

Ryan watched me closely, hopefully.

"Mr. Gambol said he is going to get Daddy out." I reached for my children's hands. "I think he can do it. He's a very important man. Now let's take a break and have some of those brownies Suzanna made last night."

I filled three glasses with milk and put brownies at the center of the table, between the schoolbooks. Quietly we ate our brownies, waiting to hear from National Security.

Fifteen minutes later, the phone rang. It was Paul Gambol. He sounded angry.

"Lissa, I called Colonel Austin and ordered him to release David, on orders from National Security. He said no! I immediately called the other members of National Security. Red lights just went off all over Washington!"

"Paul, if red lights are all that went off, then you've lost control of the military."

"Just wait! We *will* get David out of this! I'll be in touch."

I sat there for a few minutes, my head in my hands. What could I do now? Yes. I would call Jill Maynard at Shoreline News & National Commentary. She would certainly want to hear *this!*

"Jill, this is Lissa McCloud."

"Hi, Lissa. What's up?"

I filled her in on the details, then added, "National Security just ordered Spires Army Medical Center to release David. They refused!"

"You're *kidding!*"

"No, I'm not."

Jill was silent for a moment. "Lissa, what is the name and phone number of the man who said no?"

"That would be Colonel Austin." I gave her his office number.

"I'm going to call Colonel Austin now. I may be able to help you. I'll call you back afterward."

"Good. And Jill? Thank you!"

Ten minutes later, Jill was on the line again. "Lissa, I called Colonel Austin. I said, 'My name is Jill Maynard of Shoreline News & National Commentary. We're doing a story on what you are doing to Dr. McCloud. I understand that National Security ordered you to release him, and you said no. Would you like to comment?'"

"What did he say?" My pulse raced.

Jill laughed. "He sputtered a bit, then he said he didn't want to comment—and he hung up. I think I shook him!"

"Great! I'll call you later and let you know what happens."

The next afternoon, David was released to return home for the night. He was back on Haldol. He had to accept that compromise in order to be free.

The children were relieved to have David back. They clung to him, sitting on the couch together. David had broken out of the trance, but he was again sedated. The psychiatrists refused to allow him to be treated by our own doctor. We still weren't out of the woods.

I called Paul Gambol and told him what had happened. He promised to keep working on freeing David. Then I called Jill and thanked her.

I saved the call to Ben until last.

As I told him what had happened, he gasped, then chuckled. "I think you've got them on the run, Lissa! I'll let you know what happens here. This should get interesting!"

Friday afternoon, Colonel Ingermann called me. I felt a deep reluctance to talk with him, but he had helped us with the IG report.

"Lissa," he said, "Colonel Barnett heard that David broke this week. When he heard it, he celebrated! He said, 'McCloud is certifiably Looney Tunes! Nobody will believe his testimony now!'" Colonel Ingermann sounded indignant.

I was too exhausted to continue the conversation. I merely said, "Thank you for telling me. I need to get back to the children." I went to the bedroom and lay down, too dazed to cry, too tired to sleep, too hurt to respond to one more kick from the enemy.

24

A COSTLY VICTORY

NOW THAT DAVID had broken, the Spires psychiatrists were eager to get an outside opinion to confirm their diagnosis. They chose a civilian psychiatrist with whom they had a good working relationship, and made an appointment for David.

I requested that David be free of Haldol for his appointment so he could speak clearly. Under the influence of the drug, he was numb and silent, speaking only in short, confusing sentences. But the psychiatrists refused to lessen the dose or allow David to be drug-free for the appointment.

The civilian psychiatrist reported that David now had major depression, but that the army psychiatrists should not attempt to treat him because of their adversarial relationship with him.

The army psychiatrists were jubilant over the diagnosis. They ignored the finding that they should not be in charge of David's care.

That week I received another call from Nancy Haven. She was frantic about her husband and needed to talk. We agreed to meet during her lunch hour.

I drove to Fort Hardin and met Nancy at the McDonalds on post. She looked tired. We ordered lunch, then sat in a quiet corner to talk.

"Lissa, Jerry has developed a severe rash. The psychiatric staff has been treating it with ointment and making obscene comments about how he must have gotten the rash!"

She didn't have to spell it out. I was well aware of the filthy things those psychiatrists and nurses told patients to taunt them.

"I requested that they send Jerry to dermatology to determine how to treat the rash, but they refused!" She began to cry. "I'm really worried, Lissa. The rash has spread down the entire front of his body. His genitals are bleeding from it! He can no longer walk. He is in a wheelchair."

"Oh, Nancy! Have you talked with the IG or JAG?"

"Yes. I spoke with the IG. But the psychiatrists aren't listening to him. This afternoon when I get off work, I'm taking Jerry downstairs to a men's room and am taking pictures of the rash. Then I'll get them blown up and use them to help get Jerry to a dermatologist."

"Let me know what happens, Nancy. I'll be praying for you both!" I clasped her hands. "Call me as soon as you can."

The next evening, Nancy called. "It worked, Lissa!"

"What happened?"

"I took the photos of Jerry's rash up to Dr. Carver's office and showed them to him. I said, 'If you don't send Jerry to dermatology this minute, I am sending these photos to my congressman and senator.'"

I laughed. "Good going! What did he say?"

"He was furious! He said I had no right to take Jerry off the ward or to take photos of him like that! *But ...* he sent Jerry down to dermatology." She grew serious. "The dermatologist took one look at the rash and said, 'This is a staph infection! This man is dying!' He put Jerry in ICU."

"Oh, Nancy!" Staph was deadly. "Is he going to be all right?"

"I don't know yet." She sighed. "But at least he's getting proper treatment now."

We talked some more about our battle to free our husbands. Nancy promised to call me with news of Jerry.

After extensive medical intervention for the staph infection, Jerry Haven finally recovered. He was then sent back to the psychiatric ward—where the psychiatrists proceeded to break him. When he was finally released ... just short of his retirement ... the psychiatrists ruled he was "unable to function in society," and they offered him disability. Because of his age and the lack of future job opportunities now that he was broken, Jerry decided to accept the disability.

Sunday dawned with a hint of warmth and blue skies. Together, our family left for church. The songs that morning lifted my heart as I sat with my hand in David's. I don't remember what the pastor said, but I remember being encouraged by his words.

After the service, a tall, middle-aged man approached. We had seen him in Sunday school, but we didn't know him well.

"Dr. McCloud, I'm Major Easton from the Fort Hardin JAG. Pastor John told me what you are going through, and I think I may be able to help."

"Oh?" David looked cautious.

"Yes. My commanding officer, Colonel Hugh, is the JAG chief. I've told him about you, and he would like to help."

"I'm not free during the day," David said. "But could Lissa meet with him?"

"I don't see why not." He hesitated, then added, "He's a good man."

"I'll call him," I said.

First thing Monday morning, I called Colonel Hugh's office. When his aide heard who I was, she asked if I could come over that afternoon. Colonel Hugh was eager to speak with me.

Leaving the children with my neighbor, I drove to the fort. I brought along all my evidence, including the IG report given me by Colonel Ingermann.

The JAG building was a small wooden structure, painted white with green trim. The interior was dim and plain. I sat on a wooden bench outside the colonel's door until he called me in.

A tall, dark-haired man opened the office door and came out. "Mrs. McCloud, I'm Colonel Hugh, the JAG chief. Please come in." He waved me into the office and offered me a chair at a simple, wooden table. Another officer was present as well. "This is Colonel Meyers, one of our lawyers."

I shook hands with them and placed my thick manila envelope of evidence on the table in front of me.

"Ma'am, I called your lawyer and informed him of your appointment. I asked if he felt he should be here to protect you husband's interests. He said he didn't think that would be necessary, that he felt you had a good grip on the case." Colonel Hugh looked uneasy. "Are you okay with this?"

"Yes," I said firmly. The last thing I wanted was to have a non-assertive ex-JAG officer trying to limit my defense of David. This was no time for caution. I needed to lay all my cards on the table.

"We've heard a little about your case from Major Easton. Would you mind telling us the whole story?"

"I would be glad to do that. First, I would like you to read my husband's Officer Evaluation Report, which his commanding officers gave him just a couple weeks before they ordered him to see the hospital psychiatrist." I opened my envelope and handed Colonel Hugh a copy of David's OER.

Both colonels leaned over the report intently, pointing out the highlights and murmuring brief comments.

"Superb judgment ... clearly communicates ..."

"Dedicated ... responsible ... highest integrity ..."

"Should be a consultant to the surgeon general ..."

When they had finished, they looked up.

"My husband's commanding officers, Colonel Aiken and Colonel Barnett, ordered him to alter and sign a stack of time cards nearly two inches high that had accrued before David arrived in the Philippines. A great deal of money was involved. This, as you know, is fraud. The amount of money involved was huge. When David refused to cooperate with this, his commanding officers began harassing him. I asked General Neil to intervene. He did, and they backed off for awhile and gave David this Officer Evaluation Report. But when General Neil left on vacation, they again began asking my husband to alter the time cards, and they asked him to provide radiological services to an unauthorized civilian agency.

"When he refused, they sent him to the staff psychiatrist, who found nothing wrong with David—but told him he must go along with the illegal activities or he would 'fall on his sword.' David reported the harassment to the Department of the Army inspector general. When his commander learned of it, he sent David to Hawaii for another psychiatric evaluation. Again, the examining psychiatrist found nothing wrong with him.

"In the meantime, Colonel Aiken was relieved of command. But Colonel Barnett continued the harassment and had David involuntarily committed to the Spires psychiatric ward, where he has been abused for five months now.

"I recently took him to see a civilian psychiatrist, a former military doctor who used to serve at Spires. He, too, found nothing wrong with David. Here is his report." I handed the JAG officers the evaluation and scathing letter from Dr. Brewer. "Since then, the army psychiatrists, with their use of drugs and harassment, finally drove David into a depression. But these doctors were the ones who did it to him. He came here mentally fit."

When the two men finished reading Dr. Brewer's report, I said, "This entire situation was perpetrated by two men who were involved in illegal activities. It is clearly a case of psychiatric retaliation ... and it is illegal, according to the Mental Health Evaluation of Members of the Armed Forces Directive." I laid the directive on the table.

"I gave the Spires hospital command a copy of this law. But they claim it has not yet been implemented, and that they don't have to obey it. I have highlighted the portions of this law that have been violated." I sat back in my chair and waited for them to read the law.

Colonel Hugh looked it over, noted the date, then returned to the third page. Pointing to item F, he leaned over to Colonel Meyers and said, "It says here that it is effective immediately." He smiled and nodded.

"I know this claim sounds unbelievable, sir," I said, "but let me show you the testimony I have gathered to support my position."

I began handing the evidence to the two JAG officers, one piece at a time. First, Major Ralston's evidence, followed by Colonel Calloway's. Then the IG report.

"Here is an IG report on Owen Army Hospital and its commanders." I placed it on the table in front of them.

The lawyers were clearly intrigued as they read the testimony.

"Look," Colonel Hugh said to Colonel Meyers. "Here's testimony from a deputy commander of administration from *before* Colonel Calloway! He confirms Calloway's statements ... See ... here:

On one occasion Colonel Aiken introduced me to the brother of the Vice President of the Philippines who worked with their hospital system. He presented me with a list of desperately needed medical supplies. I stated that we could not legally do anything to help. Colonel Aiken requested that I price out the listing and give them what I could. I told him I would price the list, but could not legally transfer any materiel to the Filipinos. The list when priced out came to over $12 million ... Colonel Aiken was constantly frustrated with me and the "bureaucratic obstacles" I was building to "prevent" transfer of materiel to the Filipino hospitals. I refused to do anything that could be illegal.

The two men became more and more intrigued as they read through the damning testimonies. When they reached the testimony of Admiral Grady's lawyer fiercely denouncing Colonel Aiken, they looked at each other, and Colonel Hugh nodded. "This is good enough for me," he said to Colonel Meyers. He looked up. "What do you want me to do for you, Mrs. McCloud?"

"I want justice!" I looked Colonel Hugh in the eye. "And I want David released from the Army Medical Corps with his medical license intact."

Colonel Hugh nodded sympathetically. "I will help you get your husband out of this situation, Mrs. McCloud. Let me speak with the Spires commander, General Martin, and see if we can't come up with a plan."

I sighed, grateful for his help, but weary from the battle. "Thank you, Colonel Hugh."

He smiled. "I will be in touch with you soon."

With that promise ringing in my ears, I walked out of the JAG office. Maybe now I would see some progress. I should tell David, I thought. He would be encouraged.

I drove to the hospital. It was a sunny day. I enjoyed the warmth on my skin after the long winter. As I walked into the hospital lobby and headed for the library, I passed the IG's office and waved. "Hi, Ben."

Ben called out, "Lissa! Come in! You won't believe what has been happening!"

I sat across the desk from Ben. "I'm on my way to see David. The JAG officers have offered to help get him out of here."

Ben smiled and laughed. "Well, add *this* to your news: The surgeon general of the army just held a conference call with the Spires command staff and General Martin. He received your petition to free David, and he was furious! He shouted, 'What in blazes are you doing to Dr. McCloud? Let him go *at once*!'" Ben's eyes opened wide and looked straight at me. "He relieved General Martin of command and is sending a new general to command the hospital, with orders to free David."

"Wow!" I shook my head, hardly able to take it in.

Ben sat there smiling.

Suddenly it all registered. The weight I had carried all those months slipped off my shoulders. Delirious joy poured over me.

"I have to go tell David!" I exclaimed.

I found him in the stacks, patiently filing books. "David! David!" I grabbed his shoulders. "The Surgeon General has relieved General Martin of command and has issued orders to free you!" I threw my arms around him, laughing and crying at the same time.

"Are you sure?"

"Yes! Yes! Yes! It's true!" I leaned back in his arms, smiling into his eyes.

A slow smile spread across his face. "Thank God." He heaved a great sigh.

When I reached home, I told the children. Ryan heaved a great sigh of relief and Suzanna jumped up and down and clapped her hands. What a day of rejoicing!

I called David's parents and told them the news. They, too, were relieved and rejoiced with us.

"Lissa," Ruth said, "God has kept you one step ahead of the devil!"

Yes. He had indeed.

25

THE BLUE MOUNTAINS
(MARCH-APRIL)

I T WAS NOW March, and freedom was shining on the horizon. The army had not yet released David, but they were handling the case with kid gloves while trying to protect themselves legally. They claimed a lot of paperwork had to be done.

When the March issue of the *Radiology Journal* arrived, David and I sat on the couch and pored through it. While he was looking to see what positions were available, I was looking for an ad I had seen in the January and February issues for work in Spruce Valley, Oregon. But the ad was not in the March issue.

I knew that was the job opening David should examine. I went to our bedroom, found the older issues, and looked up the ad. I walked back to the living room with the magazine.

"David, I think you should contact this one." I pointed to the ad.

He shook his head. "But it's not in the March issue."

"I know. But I think it's the right one."

"I will contact that one, too. But there's an ad for a clinic in Washington, and I think I should check it out."

He sat back and sighed. "Lissa, I don't know how anyone will hire me now. When they ask for my last place of work, I'll have to say I was assigned to the psychiatric ward and worked in the hospital library."

"David, it will be okay," I said. "God has brought us this far. I know he has a plan for our future." The Jeremiah 29:11 verse ran through my head, reminding me that God's plans for us were for good and not for evil, to give us a future and a hope. I trusted his word. "I know in my heart that the ad I showed you is the right place."

"I'll put together my resume, send it out to both places, and see what comes of it," David said. "But I won't lie about what has happened to me—and I don't want you hiding the truth, either."

"Okay, David."

That night, as I lay in bed praying, I whispered to God, "Please, Father, let David get one of these jobs. His confidence is gone. I don't think he can handle a long search."

David sent his applications off that week.

A week later, a doctor from the Washington clinic called while David was at the hospital library. The command had not yet freed him, but we knew it was only a matter of time.

Following my husband's request, I told the physician what David had just experienced at the hands of the military.

The doctor said, "Mrs. McCloud, I cannot offer your husband the job under these circumstances. Please take my advice and do not tell this to anyone else, or your husband will never find work!"

When David came home that night, I told him about the conversation and the advice. His face was solemn. "Lissa, we must be honest about what happened. I will not take any job under false pretenses." He wrapped his arms around me, and I relaxed against his chest.

"Okay, David. I agree with you. I believe God will honor you because you have honored him. I'm not worried."

The next afternoon, a physician from Spruce Valley called. I also told him what David had just experienced. This time, the doctor was not so quick to withdraw the offer.

"Let me speak with my chief of staff and get back to you," he said. "I would like to speak with David, too."

That evening, the physician talked with David for a long time. The next day the doctor called me again. "Mrs. McCloud, tell your husband that we are keeping the position open for him for as long as it takes him to get free of the military. I, too, have experienced some retaliatory attacks during my career. The job is his. We are telling all other applicants that the position is filled."

Wow! God had surely answered my prayer. This was a complete shot in the dark, based only on a strong sense of God's leading—and God had just confirmed it. This was no coincidence. It was another God-thing.

The military took its time releasing David. The psychiatrists remained insistent that they were in the right. Even with a new commander, they held onto control. The other doctors, including the new general, didn't understand psychiatry. So the psychiatrists got away with bullying David, forcing him to take Haldol and using the threat of putting him back on the ward to ensure his cooperation. They told the command that it was for David's own good, that he was at risk if he didn't take the drug.

Even after all they had done to him, the Spires command was unhappy that David was not paying back the time they thought he owed the army for medical school! They refused to release him until June—and they felt he still owed them a year of service as a physician, since he had been a patient during most of his last year in the military.

It didn't make sense. The command was in trouble with the surgeon general of the army, the Subcommittee on National Security, and the press—but they held onto what they considered their rights, sucking the life out of David. The new commander was "investigating" the situation.

When April came, David was permitted to take leave to interview at the Oregon hospital. He stopped taking Haldol a few days before the trip so his hands wouldn't shake and he could think clearly again. He would be far from the psychiatrists who would slap him back in the hospital in a second if they could see he wasn't taking the drugs they had prescribed.

We left the children with Dawn and her family, our friends across the street, for a few days and boarded a plane going west. That evening, with the sky fading into gold and violet, we arrived in a wide valley surrounded by tall, blue mountain ranges capped with snow. From our motel room, we stood together and drank in the peaceful beauty.

Early the next day, David left to interview at the hospital and to meet with the chief of radiology. He would be gone most of the morning, so I explored the quaint shops in town, meeting the pleasant shopkeepers and a few customers.

When he returned, David took me to lunch at a homey restaurant with a great view of the mountains. Happiness beamed from his eyes as he told me about the new job and the doctor with whom he would be working.

I thought of how the Lord had led us through a fiery trial, a battle that had demanded every bit of our strength and courage, and how he had now brought us to this lovely, quiet place where we could recover.

"Tonight we're invited to the chief of staff's home for dinner," David said. "I know you will like Dr. Saunders, the chief of radiology, and Dr. Claussen, the chief of staff. They are both very nice."

I looked at David's shining face and felt assured that this was the right place for him.

That evening, we drove up to Dr. Claussen's house, a beautiful Victorian home with twinkly yellow lights on the porch and lace curtains at the windows.

"Come in! Come in!" said Dr. Claussen, a tall, blonde middle-aged man. He waved us inside, where the smell of roast beef and apple pie filled the air. His wife, a cheerful, round woman, smiled from the kitchen and beckoned to me.

I joined Mrs. Claussen. "What can I do?" I looked around at the serving dishes laden with food.

"You can talk to me," she said. "Tell me about yourself!"

Soon Dr. Saunders and his wife were at the door, cheerful smiles lighting their faces. They were both nearing retirement age.

It was a delightful evening, getting to know new friends and learning about the town and the hospital, a small building nestled in the foothills. Over dessert, Dr. Claussen said, "David, I am an Army Medical Corps reserve doctor. I have worked with your former commander in the Philippines. He is an immoral man. I have heard stories … and I know he has done the same thing to others as he has done to you. We will help you rebuild."

We were speechless. Finally, David managed to thank Dr. Claussen for his generosity.

There is no way David could have blindly applied to any job and landed in a place where the chief of staff knew all about his former commander—and was willing to help David rebuild. It was another God-thing.

But God was not finished surprising us.

The next day, David and I went to a real estate agent to see if we could line up a house to rent beginning in June. "We are looking for a rental," David said. "But if you should by chance show us our dream house, we will buy it."

The agent took us around the town and showed us a few places that were available, but we weren't wild about any of them.

Finally, David held up a housing magazine that featured a picture of a log home. "Could you show us this house?"

The agent looked at the ad. "Dr. McCloud," he said, "this house is many miles from your workplace. I don't think you would want to live there."

"Could we see it anyway?"

"Okay," he said reluctantly.

We drove across the valley, toward the blue mountains. In the foothills, we arrived at the back of a log home. As I stepped from the car, a gentle breeze touched my cheeks, a breeze scented with pine.

The agent unlocked the back door and ushered us into the house.

We walked down the hallway, through a beautiful, big kitchen, and out into the living room. A cathedral ceiling rose above our heads. Before us were two giant picture windows. Outside, a deck ran around the house. Through the windows I saw pine trees rising from the slope below the house. Off to the side I heard water bubbling over rocks. In what seemed like slow motion, I turned and looked behind me. An open staircase rose to a loft bedroom—just like the one in my dream.

A shiver ran up my back, and goose bumps covered my arms. I turned to David and whispered, "David! I'm standing in that dream!" It was exactly what I had seen, heard, and felt that night in January, when God had shown me the place he was preparing for us.

David looked into my eyes, then turned to the agent and said, "We'll buy it."

On the way back into town, I saw a billboard along the highway. It simply said:

I have loved you with an everlasting love.

—God

I cannot describe the awe and joy that filled my heart. Tears cascaded down my cheeks. I felt that Jesus was towering over the valley, smiling—his hand opened over this incredible gift.

Coincidence? Not remotely possible!

26

WALKING OFF THE BATTLEFIELD
(MAY-JUNE)

T HE BATTLE WAS not yet finished. Back in Oklahoma, we still had to negotiate David's release from the military. David entrusted the negotiations mostly to me, since he was emotionally exhausted.

Again, I found myself in the JAG office. This time, the JAG chief had an offer to put on the table.

"We are prepared to send David monthly disability checks in the amount of $900 for five years. At any time during those five years, we can call him back to duty so he can finish repaying his medical school loan."

This was not justice! Not remotely. A red flag waved in my mind, and several points seemed to shout. First, David's confidence was very shaky. If he were to receive monthly disability checks, he would feel disabled and would lose his courage. Second, the military had battered him to the point of breaking, and he was now on powerful drugs. This offer of money could be viewed as a settlement on their part. If so, it was an insulting amount for what they had done. Third, if we accepted this deal, David could be recalled to active duty in the Army Medical Corps, the institution that had tried to destroy him. Fourth, if we settled, we would no longer have any grounds for legal action.

I looked up at Colonel Hugh and said, "No."

The colonel looked startled.

"Colonel Hugh," I said, "if the army sends David a disability check, I will tear it up and send it back! Your money is dirty. If we accept it, we agree that what you did to him was right. And it wasn't! If we accept this deal, it means I will shut up about what happened here, and I won't! I want David's separation from the military to be final, as though an employer and an employee agreed to part ways with no strings attached. This is not justice! I will not accept this deal. But I *will* see you in court!"

"Mrs. McCloud, your husband still owes the army for his medical school training."

"After what was done to him?" I was incredulous. "I want him to be totally free of the military, with no further obligation!"

Colonel Hugh looked blank. "We have never handled anything like this before! We don't even have such a form!"

"Then make one up," I said. "Let me know when you have drawn it up, and I will have our lawyer review it." I walked out of his office, indignant that the army thought it could buy us off.

When the JAG officers finally designed the release form, they demanded that David agree to pay them back for the remaining time owed to the army for his medical school training.

I did not want to accept it; this was coercion. But David wanted out from under the army's rule. He wanted it badly. "We'll take the deal," he said.

After David signed the papers, I went to Ben's office and told him about it.

"Lissa," he said, "I will do everything I can to make them drop the requirement that David pay them back for his training. This is just wrong!"

"Thank you, Ben." I breathed a sigh of relief. "You have been a great help."

The next weeks seemed to drag as we waited for David to be free of the military. By the time David signed out, he had severe palsy from the Haldol. His entire body shook as he signed the final papers releasing him. But he was forced to take the drug until the day he was officially released.

Finally, we arrived at our last day in Oklahoma. We had rented a large truck to move our household goods west. It stood in the driveway, packed to the ceiling.

Flowers bloomed around the house, and the lawn had turned green. The sun was hot. But compared to the Philippines that time of year, it was pleasant. Through the long winter, we had not adjusted to the cold, so we basked in the summer's warmth.

We had cleaned the house. Now it was time for a final walk-through. I examined each room, opened drawers and cupboards, checking windows and making sure there were no grubby child-level fingerprints anywhere in the house. Then I reached the master bathroom.

I had forgotten to pack the trash pail. I reached down to pick it up—and froze. In the bottom lay the Haldol, all David's medals, and the oak leaf insignias he had worn on his uniform.

Tears rushed to my eyes as I felt his betrayal and the depth of his pain. I straightened up, still staring into the trash. Through the blur of tears, I remembered the promotion ceremony at Letterman Army Medical Center the day David became a major. I remembered my pride as I had pinned those oak leaves on one shoulder of his uniform, while the commanding general had pinned the other. I remembered how pleased David had been to have finally completed his medical specialty training.

Now the oak leaves lay in the trash can, discarded by the brave man who had spent so many years earning them.

Suzanna came into the room and saw me looking into the garbage.

I wiped the tears from my eyes, not wanting to upset her.

She walked over to the pail and leaned over, her brown head coming between the trash and me. She stood still a moment, then reached down and rescued the oak leaves. Holding them in her palm, her face solemn and her eyes huge, she asked, "Mama, can I wear these for Daddy?"

"Yes, honey." I folded her into my arms, my tears dropping onto her hair.

I disposed of the trash and pushed the pail into the back of the truck. David shut the door, then enveloped me in his arms. "We're free at last, honey," he whispered. "Let's go home."

David climbed into the moving van, with Ryan and Freckles to keep him company. I climbed into David's truck, Suzanna at my side.

We left Oklahoma that day, never to return, and headed toward the blue mountains and the home God had provided for us. Our battle was finished. It was time to move forward into the place of blessing.

For years afterward, Suzanna wore David's oak leaves on her jacket collar, in honor of her father's service to his country. When others asked why she wore them, she always said, "I'm wearing these for my Daddy."

EPILOG

YEARS HAVE PASSED since these events. Our children have grown into fine adults who love and trust the Lord, and they now have families of their own. David and I still live in Spruce Valley, that lovely town in the western mountains.

Colonel Erickson, from Admiral Grady's staff, resigned his commission because of what was done to David. Several other officers also resigned, including Major Ben Duggan, who kept in touch with us at Christmas for a few years after David was released.

I would like to be able to say that we all lived happily ever after. But life is not like that. Life is messy, as Ryan reminds me. God brings us through journeys that seem to make no sense. Yet, though we can rarely see it from his viewpoint, there is always a design, always a plan.

When our family arrived at the blue mountains of my dream, I felt relief. But it was short-lived. In the nightmare, I had to return to the swamp to try to save my husband. And so it was in real life.

David and I did not fully understand the chemical imbalance caused by the forced use of Haldol. A month after he stopped taking it, he again had a breakdown. It took a week to get back on his feet. It devastated him to realize his battle was not yet over.

I returned to the swamp—the swamp of trying to free David from the effects of retaliation, to help him regain his self-confidence and dignity. Yes, he was free from military captivity. But would he ever recover?

A civilian doctor diagnosed David with post-traumatic stress disorder (PTSD) caused by the psychiatric abuse. He gave David a different drug, trying to wean him off all medications. But the damage done by the Army Medical Corps was permanent. It had created a chemical imbalance that would always need to be treated. That was a huge blow for us both to absorb.

During this time, David also had other medical tests. He was diagnosed with hepatitis C, an illness that plagues medical workers who are exposed to many different diseases in their course of work. It required aggressive treatment. Clearly, this was the illness from which he had suffered the entire time the army psychiatrists were pumping him with harmful drugs. Those drugs had made his illness worse.

In sorting through David's medical records, we could find no test that ever explored the reason for his jaundice—though all forms of hepatitis would have been the first area the doctors in the Philippines and Oklahoma should have explored. It was an elementary first step. Every military doctor had ignored the obvious. But David did not want to file a lawsuit. His emotions were too raw; he needed time to heal.

Shortly after we arrived in Spruce Valley, our military attorney friend Brian Newall sent us a copy of a new law the JAG had just finished. He was a member of the team that wrote it. Brian said that among themselves, the JAG members who wrote it called it "David's Law." Formally, it was entitled "Military Whistleblower Protection." (See Appendix B.) It now stands as a guardian for those in the military who wish to serve with honor, and it was the direct result of David's battle. This was his victory.

But David himself was hurt too deeply to appreciate the great thing God had done through him. He was broken. Slowly, ever so slowly, he fought his way back toward wholeness, but the battle was arduous.

When the Department of the Army inspector general's office finally released the results of its investigation—eighteen months after David was released— they concluded that, yes, David's rights had been violated—but it was for his own good, since he was "mentally ill." Never mind that he was involuntarily admitted to the psychiatric ward after being found mentally fit by two army psychiatrists. Never mind that an outside psychiatrist had declared him fit. Never mind that it took five months for the psychiatrists at Spires Army Medical Center to break him to get their diagnosis!

It was a tacit admission of guilt, but the military was claiming they weren't *really* guilty because their self-investigation had rearranged the facts to suit their story, to protect their legal backside. It was a whitewash.

That same month, the Department of Defense sent David a bill for well over $8,000 for the food he ate during his stay at Spires Army Medical Center.

When the bill arrived, it threw David into a serious breakdown. He lay on the couch in an almost catatonic state for three months, speaking only when he must. He resigned his job, for he could no longer focus. We suddenly found ourselves with no income and no safety net.

Two months later, I looked at that enormous, deadly bill, which had now grown. Each month we did not pay, a fine was levied against us. I sat at the table one morning, staring at the bill, wondering how to pay it with no income. Fury at this continuing injustice rose in my spirit. I could no longer tolerate the military's relentless pursuit. Not content to destroy David, now they were coming after the income we did not have! Under my breath I vowed, "I will *never* pay this bill!"

It was time to fight back, no holds barred.

I knew we would need an ex-JAG to fight the Department of Defense. After doing some research, I discovered there were only two ex-JAG officers in our area. The men had set up shop in a city two hours away. I made an appointment to see one, taking with me a power of attorney from David, plus all our documentation.

It was snowing the day I drove to see the lawyer. I was nervous. Would either of these veterans believe our story? I entered the office building, shook the snow off my coat, and knocked on their office door. A tall young man greeted me. "Come in. You must be Mrs. McCloud." He introduced himself and invited me to sit by his desk.

At first, the lawyer was skeptical of my account. But as I laid the evidence before him, his face grew red with indignation until he could hardly contain himself. What the military had done was a betrayal of all he believed.

Finally, he said, "Mrs. McCloud, we can file suit against the military for this. But I must warn you that the military enjoys sovereign immunity. That means we can sue, but they can decide whether or not to hear the case. This status they enjoy is the result of a Supreme Court ruling that has resulted in what is known as the Feres Doctrine."

This did not stop me. I told the lawyer, "I have called the reporter who helped get David out of the army. I want to file a lawsuit against the Department of Defense and the army. As soon as we file suit, the reporter will release our story. She has been saving it for the right time. After she releases it, she is handing it off to the national televised press. We *will* make the military back down! We *will* make them take back this bill."

And that is exactly what happened.

We filed the suit. The story went national in the press, both written and televised. Nancy and Jerry Haven's story was shown at the same time as ours, making the evidence very powerful.

The press filed to receive a copy of the IG report on our case. Because of the Freedom of Information Act, they were able to obtain it. The reporter who helped us said, "Lissa, this case is the most well-documented, clear-cut, blatant case of retaliation we in the press have ever seen. When we heard the news about the Department of the Army inspector general report, the news room erupted. People were jumping around shouting, 'We've got them! We've finally got them!'

"The press has known for many years that the military puts whistle-blowers through psychiatric retaliation," the reporter said, "but we've never had enough evidence until now to expose them."

Before the story was televised, the secretary of the army called me. We spoke on the phone with our lawyers present, in a stilted, careful exchange of information. That evening, I found her number by dialing information. I called her at her home and we spoke woman to woman. During that conversation, I learned she had asked a Pentagon physician to search David's medical records. He confirmed what we had discovered: The tests confirmed abnormally high bilirubin, and the records showed David suffered from fever. But no tests were conducted to discover the cause of the jaundice or fever, either in the Philippines or at Spires Army Medical Center.

After talking for some time, the secretary of the army said, "Mrs. McCloud, I personally believe that what happened to your husband was a conspiracy cover-up. Nobody told me about this until the media called and asked for my comment. The military doctors are supposed report to me! Yet they told me nothing of this. But while I believe this was a conspiracy cover-up, I will never admit that publicly because of my position with the army."

She told me she wished to settle our case and to see David compensated. But she was dismissed from her position before she could arrange a settlement.

When interviewed by a television host who told of our struggle for justice, the secretary of the army said the military had not *intentionally* broken the law, an admission that it had done so. The host was quick to catch the admission. The secretary of the army came very near to apologizing to us on that national news program. It was the closest thing to an apology we ever received from the army.

The military refused to hear our case, and there was never any settlement or compensation. But the Department of Defense withdrew the bill it had sent to David. By the time the bill was dismissed, it had grown to nearly $10,000. Almost $2,000 in fines had been levied against David in just a few short months because of his failure to pay.

And what of the military officers who did this to David? I heard from Colonel Duffy that some very high-ranking officers involved in our case, men who knowingly allowed David to suffer psychiatric retaliation, faced disciplinary action. But others went on to gain power and recognition within the Army Medical Corps. But none of this was ever made public; the military does not lay itself open to lawsuits by admitting guilt.

Meanwhile, I had children to feed and a husband who could not work. He was too ill for me to leave him alone, so I couldn't work, either. We lived far from town and had no money. The fight to free David had drained our resources. What could I do?

My pastor told me, "Lissa, we will help you with your children while you try to get David back on his feet." My pastor was the man from the hut in my dream. He and a small group of Christians helped me raise Ryan and Suzanna while I struggled to help David, who had grown silent. This small group of people became in many ways our extended family, filling the gaps left by David's withdrawal.

The year David couldn't work, friends from all over the country sent us money to help. A bill would arrive and before it was due, a check would arrive from a friend, accompanied by a note that said, "God asked me to send this to you." Our hearts were greatly blessed by this tremendous show of support and friendship.

Our pastor also saw that David needed to do some kind of work to recover from his debilitating illness. So he asked a man from church who owned an oil and lube shop to hire David.

The man and his family welcomed us to their business team and helped David get back on his feet. All David could do was vacuum cars that were brought in for servicing. The pay was very small, but it was something, and the work helped him regain some confidence. It gave him the courage to look for work in the medical field.

It took many years for David to pull out of the depression that settled on his spirit. His wonderful, godly character remained constant, but his vibrant personality disappeared as he battled post-traumatic stress disorder and the chemical imbalance. He became silent, shy around others, unsure of himself. I was not able to save him from the effects of the battle he had fought.

Over the years, David has gradually opened up again. He found work as a physician, determining people's disabilities for a government agency.

It is a desk job and does not involve patient care. Because of his lack of confidence, he never returned to medical practice. During the first ten years of recovery, he rarely talked. But lately his dry sense of humor has surfaced, and I have delighted in it. David enjoys his work, for through it he is able to help others in need. He also has some good friends among his co-workers. He is content to be where he is.

You may ask, "And what about you, Lissa?"

Trauma and trials change people. Some say, "God did not protect me, so from now on, I will take care of things myself." They grow hard and bitter—and want nothing to do with a God they feel let them down. They also become hard toward the suffering of those around them.

But others say, "God allowed this to happen to me. I don't understand why, but I know he loves me, because he sent his only Son to die for me, to save me. So I choose to trust him. He alone is the source of all healing."

I will not pretend this choice is easy. It is incredibly difficult! Yet that was the path I chose. I did not want to become bitter and cold, useless to God.

Life is full of pain. It's what we do with that pain that either cripples or strengthens us. If we focus on our own hurt, we grow bitter. Bitterness is the fiery whip of the devil that wraps itself around our feet and pulls us down into darkness. It isolates us from the healing power of Jesus, the Great Physician. But if we focus on Jesus, we are healed by his love. He cuts through the whip of bitterness and sets us free.

It took me three years to overcome my initial anger at the army for the damage it had done to David. It took a daily surrendering of my circumstances to God for me to move forward. It took my forgiving the people who had destroyed David. I knew I would find no peace in my heart until I let the anger go.

Fortunately, God gave me a pastor who prayed for me through this battle of emotions. He prayed that I would come to know the height and depth and width of God's love for me. He stood by our family and held us up while we struggled to survive the emotional turmoil of David's health battle and our changing circumstances.

I'm still learning about God's great love. Through the difficult years, I have leaned on him. The harder life became, the harder I leaned on Jesus. He has given me joy in the midst of suffering, hope in the face of disaster, and kindness toward others who suffer. He has kept my soul close to his heart. He has filled my heart with laughter!

I have come to know Jesus better than I ever imagined possible. He is my Beloved. I would not trade the suffering of this trial for a lifetime of ease. For through suffering, I have learned in the depths of my soul that Jesus' abiding presence and love are worth far more than anything earth could offer.

From the vantage point of years, I can now see why God allowed that horrific experience. This life isn't just about me or about those I love. There is a bigger picture that only God can see. Though most military officers we have known have been honorable, David's commanding officers in the Philippines and the doctors at Spires AMC were not. And they were not the only ones to abuse psychiatry. During this battle, I learned that David was one of many thousands who have suffered in this manner.

God saw what was happening to honorable men and women at the hands of unscrupulous commanders and psychiatrists. So he sent two of his own children into the situation. Through our battle, he brought this horrific practice to light. He gave us friends in significant positions, friends who would write a law to protect our service men and women from abusive commanding officers.

This law did not completely end psychiatric retaliation. There will always be lawless men in any organization who will try to manipulate people. But now the law can provide protection for military members who find themselves in the same situation as David. It can help others escape the same fate.

That was God's purpose in our battle. I am content to be used for that end.

What we have lived through has not been easy. But sometimes there are unexpected blessings, like the weekend we visited Suzanna and her husband in Alaska.

We attended an open-air farmers' market the Saturday morning before the Fourth of July. White tents stood on the misty slope between the town and the bay. We walked among the booths together, enjoying the smell of the sea mingled with hotdogs and sausage.

Then a voice spoke over the loudspeaker, announcing a woman would sing the Star-Spangled Banner to open the market that day. The flag was raised at one side of the marketplace. As the music soared through the air in piercing sweetness, my throat tightened. For those of us who love America and have sacrificed for our country, the flag represents both the love and the loss. Whenever that anthem sounds, my hand goes to my heart—and tears flood my eyes as I remember the terrible price David and so many others have paid for freedom.

EPILOG

But this time I paused and studied the people in the Alaskan marketplace, curious to see the reactions of those around me, to observe my daughter's world. Standing between Suzanna and David, I watched as the early morning shoppers stopped and faced the flag. Some saluted. Some put their hands over their hearts.

From the corner of my eye I saw Suzanna's youthful hand slide over her heart, this daughter who had rescued her father's oak leaves and had worn them in his honor.

David was watching her, too. He hesitated a few seconds, his head bowed. Then he lifted his eyes and faced the flag. Slowly, his trembling hand came up to cover his heart … for the first time since he had thrown away those oak leaves.

Standing by the sea with my hand over my heart, I felt a wave of tears well up, pour down my cheeks, and wash through my soul.

It was a healing moment, a moment to treasure.

And I smiled.

ONE STEP AHEAD OF THE DEVIL
A SONG LISSA WROTE BASED ON
EPHESIANS 6:10-18

Born to be a warrior, born to serve a King,
Given strength from childhood ... he trained me for this thing.
Destined to wear his armor, given ground to hold,
At his call step forward, in his strength I'm bold!

Helmet of salvation ... Spirit be my Sword ...
Righteousness my breastplate ... my armor from the Lord.
Chosen to spread the good news in a world of sin,
Truth of God's salvation, precious souls to win ...

(chorus)

One step ahead of the devil, out front where the battle lies,
"Warrior of Christ, in the shield of faith, stand firm in the gap!" he
cries.
Well there ain't no armor for the backside, brother!
You'd better not turn and run!
We're gonna take this land for Jesus,
Gonna stand in the gap until he comes!

This song was recorded by Paul Barber.
You may listen to it at www.polebaba.com.

APPENDIX A

DEPARTMENT OF DEFENSE

DIRECTIVE

September 14, 1993
NUMBER 6490.1

(This is the original law in effect at the time of these events. To see current law, search on-line: Department of Defense Directive Number 6490.1, October 1, 1997)

SUBJECT: Mental Health Evaluations of Members of the Armed Forces

Reference:

(a) Public Law 101-510, "National Defense Authorization Act for Fiscal Year 1991" November 5, 1990
(b) Public Law 102-484, "National Defense Authorization Act for Fiscal Year 1993," October 23, 1992
(c) DoD Directive 7050.6, "Military Whistleblower Protection," September 3, 1992
(d) National Center for State Courts' Guidelines through for Involuntary Civil Commitment, 1986
(e) through (i), see enclosure 1

A. PURPOSE

This Directive:

1. Implements congressional requirements in references (a) and (b) to:

   (a) Establish the rights of members referred by their commands for mental health evaluations.
   (b) Establish procedures for outpatient and inpatient mental health evaluations that provide protection to members referred by their commands for such evaluations.

2. Prohibits the use of referrals by commands for mental health evaluations in reprisal against whistleblowers for disclosures protected by references (b) and (c).
3. Incorporates into DoD procedures information in references (d) through (f) that contain guidelines on psychiatric hospitalization of adults prepared by professional civilian health organizations.

B. APPLICABILITY AND SCOPE

This Directive applies to:

1. The Office of the Secretary of Defense, the Military Departments (including the National Guard), the Chairman of the Joint Chiefs of Staff and the Joint Staff, the Inspector General of the Department of Defense (IG, DoD), and the DoD Field Activities (hereafter referred to collectively as "the DoD Components").
2. The procedures for referral for mental health evaluation of members of the Armed Forces in situations OTHER THAN those related to responsibility and competence inquiries conducted pursuant to Rule for Court-Martial 706 of MCM, 1983 (reference (g)).

C. DEFINITIONS:

Terms used in this Directive are defined in enclosure 2.

D. POLICY

It is DoD policy that:

1. A commanding officer shall consult with a mental health professional before referring a member for mental health evaluation to be conducted on an outpatient basis. (See enclosure 3.)
2. A member has certain rights when referred for a mental health evaluation and additional rights when admitted to a treatment facility for an emergency or involuntary mental health evaluation. (See enclosure 3.)
3. No person shall refer a member for mental health evaluation as a reprisal for making or preparing a lawful communication to a Member of Congress, any appropriate authority in the chain of command of the member, an inspector general (IG), or a member of a DoD audit, inspection, investigation, or law enforcement organization.
4. No person shall restrict a member from lawfully communicating with an IG, attorney, Member of Congress, or others about the member's referral for a mental health evaluation.
5. Any violation of subsections D.3. or D.4., above, by any person subject to the UCMJ (reference (h)) is punishable in accordance with the provisions of paragraphs E.4. a. below. Any violation of these subsections by a civilian employee is punishable under regulations governing civilian disciplinary or adverse actions.
6. Nothing in these procedures shall be construed to limit the authority of a commander to refer members for emergency mental-health evaluation and/or treatment when circumstances suggest the need for such action.

E. RESPONSIBILITIES

1. The Assistant Secretary of Defense (Personnel and Readiness) shall exercise oversight for compliance with this Directive on personnel issues.
2. The Assistant Secretary of Defense (Health Affairs) shall exercise oversight for compliance with this Directive on mental health services.
3. The Inspector General of the Department of Defense shall:

   a. Conduct or oversee an investigation of an allegation submitted to an IG that the member was referred for a mental health evaluation in violation of this Directive.

    b.   Include assessments reported to him or her that a mental health evaluation was used in violation of this Directive in the IG's semiannual report to the Congress.

4.   The Secretaries of the Military Departments shall:

    a.   Within 120 days of the date of this Directive, publish an implementing regulation that provides that violations of the prohibitions referenced in subsections D.3. or D.4., above, by persons subject to the UCMJ (reference (h)) are punishable as a violation of Article 92 of the UCMJ (reference (h)), and that such violations by civilian employees are punishable under regulations governing civilian disciplinary or adverse actions.

    b.   Ensure that commanders are knowledgeable about their responsibility for ensuring that members are not referred for mental health evaluations as reprisal for whistleblowing; commanders follow the requirements in enclosure 3; and commanders shall consult with mental health professionals before referring members for mental health evaluations.

    c.   Establish procedures for reporting any assessments that a mental health evaluation was used in a manner in violation of this Directive to the IG, DoD.

F. EFFECTIVE DATE AND IMPLEMENTATION

This Directive is effective immediately. The Military Departments shall forward two copies of implementing documents to the Assistant Secretary of Defense (Personnel and Readiness) within 120 days.

William J. Perry
Deputy Secretary of Defense

Enclosures—3
    1.   References
    2.   Definitions
    3.   Mental Health Evaluation Requirements

APPENDIX A

REFERENCES, continued

(Encl. 1)

(e) The American Psychiatric Association's Task Force Report, "Involuntary Commitment to Outpatient Treatments," 1987

(f) The American Psychiatric Association's Report, "Guidelines for Legislation on the Psychiatric Hospitalization of Adults," 1983

(g) Manual for Courts-Martial, United States, 1984

(h) Chapter 47 of title 10, United States Code, "Uniform Code of Military Justice" (UCMJ)

(i) The American Psychiatric Association, "Diagnostic and Statistical Manual of Mental Disorders" (Third Edition, revised), 1987

DEFINITIONS

(Encl. 2)

1. Communicating. "Communication" means a communication in which a member of the armed forces makes a complaint or discloses information that a member reasonably believes constitutes evidence of: (a) a violation of a law or regulation or (b) mismanagement, a gross waste of funds, an abuse of authority, or a substantial and specific danger to public health and safety.

2. Emergency. An "emergency" or involuntary admission for a mental health evaluation may occur when an individual is found by a privileged mental health provider, to be suffering from a mental disorder that makes the individual a danger to self, to others, or to government property.

3. Inspector General (IG). The Inspector General, DoD, and a military or civilian employee assigned or detailed under DoD Component regulations to serve as an IG at any command level in one of the DoD Components.

4. Least Restrictive Alternative Principle. A principle under which a member of the Armed Forces committed for hospitalization and treatment shall be placed in the most appropriate and therapeutic available setting that is no more restrictive than is conducive to the most effective form of treatment, and in which treatment is available and the risks of physical injury or property damage posed by such a placement are warranted by the proposed plan of treatment.

5. Member. Any member of the Army, the Navy, the Air Force, or the Marine Corps.

6. Mental Disorder. As defined by the Diagnostic and Statistical Manual of Mental Disorders (reference (i)), a mental disorder is: "A clinically significant behavioral or psychological syndrome or pattern that occurs in a person that is associated with present distress (a painful symptom) or disability (impairment in one or more important areas of functioning) or with a significantly increased risk of suffering death, pain, disability, or an important loss of freedom. In addition, this syndrome or pattern must not be merely an expectable response to a particular event; e.g., the death of a loved one. Whatever its original cause, it must currently be considered a manifestation of a behavioral, psychological, or biological dysfunction in the person. Neither deviant behavior; e.g., political, religious, or sexual, nor conflicts that are primarily between the individual and society are mental disorders unless the deviance or conflict is a symptom of a dysfunction in the person, as described above."

7. Mental Health Evaluation. A psychiatric examination or evaluation, a psychological examination or evaluation, an examination for psychiatric or psychological fitness for duty, or any other means of assessing a member's state of mental health. It does not include interviews about family advocacy programs or Services for drug and alcohol abuse rehabilitation programs.

8. Mental Health Professional. A psychiatrist or clinical psychologist, a person with a doctorate in clinical social work, or a psychiatric clinical nurse specialist with appropriate credentials who are properly privileged to conduct mental health evaluations for DoD activities.

MENTAL HEALTH EVALUATION REQUIREMENTS

(Encl. 3)

1. Referrals for outpatient and inpatient (other than in an emergency) evaluation.

   a. When a commander determines it is necessary to refer a member for a mental health evaluation, the commander shall first consult with a mental health professional and then shall ensure that the member is provided with a written notice of the referral. The notice shall, AT A MINIMUM, include the following:

(1) The date and time the mental health evaluation is scheduled.

(2) A brief factual description of the behaviors and/or verbal expressions that caused the commander to determine a mental health evaluation is necessary.

(3) The name or names of the mental health professionals with whom the commanding officer has consulted before making the referral. If such consultation is not possible, the notice shall include reason why.

(4) The positions and telephone numbers of authorities, including attorneys and IGs, who can assist a member who wishes to question the referral.

(5) The member must be provided with a copy of the rights listed in paragraph 1.b. of this enclosure, below.

(6) The member's signature attesting to having received the notice described in subparagraphs 1.a. (1) through (5) of this enclosure, above. If the member refuses to sign the attestation, the commander shall so indicate on the notice.

b. Member's Rights. In any case in which a member of the Armed Forces is referred for a mental health evaluation, other than in an emergency, the following provisions apply:

(1) Upon the request of the member, an attorney who is a member of the Armed Forces or employed by the Department of Defense and who is designated to provide advice under this section shall advise the member of the ways in which the member may seek redress.

(2) If a member of the Armed Services submits to an IG an allegation that the member was referred for a mental health evaluation in violation of this Directive or implementing Directives, the IG, DoD, shall conduct or oversee an investigation of the allegation.

(3) The member shall have the right to also be evaluated by a mental health professional of the member's own choosing if reasonably available. Any such evaluation, including an evaluation by a mental health professional who is not an employee of the Department of Defense, shall be conducted within a reasonable period of time after the member is referred for an evaluation and shall be at the member's own expense.

(4) No person may restrict the member in communicating with an IG, attorney, Member of Congress, or others about the member's referral for a mental health evaluation. This provision does not apply to a communication that is unlawful.

(5) In situations other than emergencies, the member shall have at least 2 business days before a scheduled mental health evaluation to meet with an attorney, IG, chaplain, or other appropriate party. If a commanding officer believes the condition of the member requires that a mental health evaluation occur sooner, the commanding officer shall state the reasons in writing as part of the request for consultation.

(6) If the member is aboard a naval vessel or in circumstances related to a member's military duties that make compliance with any of the procedures in subsection 1. of this enclosure, above, impractical, the commanding officer seeking the referral shall prepare a memorandum stating the reasons for the inability to comply with such procedures.

c. Upon request by a member for advice from an attorney, an attorney shall be appointed at no cost to the member to advise the member of ways in which they may seek redress (including, but not limited to, Article 138 of the UCMJ (reference (h)). In those instances where an attorney is not reasonably available, the Services shall specify an alternative source of advice, typically the local IG. IGs shall investigate allegations that a member received inadequate advice regarding the member's rights under this Directive or means to seek redress; and shall ensure action to resolve complaints of wrong against commanding officers. Complaints about judge advocate shall be referred to the appropriate representative of the Service's Department of the Judge Advocate General.

d. During the outpatient mental health evaluation, the mental health professionals shall assess the circumstances surrounding the request for a mental health evaluation to ensure that the evaluation does not appear to have been used as a reprisal for whistleblowing. Evidence that indicates that the evaluation may have been requested inappropriately shall be reported by the mental health professional through his or her command channels to the superiors of the referring commander. Additionally, the mental health professionals shall also ensure that members are advised of the purpose, nature, and likely consequences of the evaluation, and make clear to the member that evaluation lacks confidentiality. When a mental health professional performs both evaluative and therapeutic roles, the possible conflict of loyalties should be clearly explained to the member-patient at the outset of the therapeutic relationship. See the Principles of Medical Ethics with Annotations Especially Applicable to Psychiatry (1989), e.g., Section 4; and the Ethical Principles of Psychologists (1992), e.g., Principle B. (Integrity), Principle D (Respect for People's Rights and Dignity) and Principle E (Concern for Other's Welfare).

2. Admissions for emergency or involuntary inpatient evaluation and additional rights of members.
   a. Inpatient mental health evaluations should be used only if and when such evaluations cannot appropriately or reasonably be conducted on an outpatient basis, in accordance with the least restrictive alternative principle. Only a psychiatrist, or, in cases in which a psychiatrist is not available, another mental health professional or physician, may admit a member of the Armed Forces for a mental health evaluation to be conducted on an inpatient basis.
   b. When a member is admitted to a treatment facility for an emergency or involuntary mental health evaluation, the following provisions apply:

      (1) Reasonable efforts shall be made, as soon after admission as the member's condition permits, to inform the member of the reasons for the evaluation, the nature and consequences of the evaluation and any treatment, and the member's rights.
      (2) The member shall have the right to contact, as soon after admission as the member's condition permits, a friend, relative, attorney or IG.
      (3) The member shall be evaluated by the attending psychiatrist or physician within 2 business days after admittance to determine if continued hospitalization and treatment is justified or if the member should be released from the facility.
      (4) If a determination is made that continued hospitalization and treatment is justified, the member must be notified orally and in writing of the reason for such determination.

(5) A review of the admission of the member and the appropriate-ness of continued hospitalization and treatment shall be conducted in accordance with paragraph 2.c. this enclosure, below.

c.   The review procedure shall be conducted as follows:

(1) Within 72 hours of an involuntary-emergency psychiatric admission initiated under this Directive, a review of the admission and of the appropriateness of continued hospital-ization shall be conducted. The review shall be conducted by an officer NOT in the member's immediate chain of command, who is neutral and disinterested, and appointed by an appropriate commander in the grade of 0-5 or above.

(2) The review procedure shall include the specified reviewer's introduction of her or himself to the member and indicate the reasons for the interview. The reviewer shall notify the member of the right to have legal representation during the review by a judge advocate, or at his own expense by an attorney of the member's choosing who is available within a reasonable time. The reviewer shall specify the length of the review process necessary before a determination regard-ing hospitalization will be rendered and the need for any subsequent reviews.

(3) The reviewer shall determine whether continued evaluation, treatment, or discharge is appropriate. This is accomplished in part by reviewing the evaluation set forth in subparagraph 2.b. (3) this enclosure, above. Also, the reviewer shall determine if there is reasonable cause to believe the referral for evaluation was used in an inappropriate, retributive, or punitive manner; that is, in violation of this Directive or implementing Service regulations. If the reviewer determines the referral was inappropriate, the reviewer shall report the finding to appropriate authorities for further investigation using the procedures established by each Service.

APPENDIX B
("DAVID'S LAW")

DEPARTMENT OF DEFENSE

DIRECTIVE

August 12, 1995
NUMBER 7050.6

(This is the original law passed in response to this case. To see current law, search online: Department of Defense Directive Number 7050.6, June 23, 2000)

SUBJECT: Military Whistleblower Protection

References:
(a) DoD Directive 7050.6, subject above, September 3, 1992 (hereby cancelled)
(b) Chapter 47 and Sections 892, 1034, 1552, and 1553 of the title 10 United States Code
(c) DoD Directive 6490.1, "Mental Health Evaluations of Members of the Armed Forces," September 14, 1993
(d) Section 552 and Appendix III of title 5, United States Code
(e) DoD Directive 5505.6, "Investigations of Allegations Against Senior Officials of the Department of Defense," July 12, 1991
(f) DoD Directive 7050.1, "Defense Hotline Program," March 20, 1987

A. REISSUANCE AND PURPOSE

This Directive reissues reference (a) to:

1. Update policy and responsibilities for military whistleblower protection under Section 1034 of reference (b).
2. Include complaints of sexual harassment or unlawful discrimination as "protected communications," as defined in enclosure 2, definition 8.
3. Expand the scope of persons and activities to whom a protected communication may be made, to include any person or organization (including any person or organization in the chain of command) designated under Component regulations or other established administrative procedures to receive such communications.
4. Include referral for mental health evaluations under reference (c) as a "personal action," as defined in enclosure 2, definition 7.

B. APPLICABILITY AND SCOPE

This Directive applies to:

1. The Office of the Secretary of Defense, the Military Departments (including the Coast Guard when it is operating as Military Service in the Navy), the Chairman of the Joint Chiefs of Staff, the Combat Commands, the Inspector General of the Department of Defense (IG, DoD), the Defense Agencies, and the DoD Field Activities, including nonappropriated fund activities (hereafter referred to collectively as "the DoD Components"). The term "Military Services," as used herein, refers to the Army, the Navy, the Air Force, and the Marine Corps.
2. All DoD personnel.

C. DEFINITIONS

Terms used in this Directive are defined in enclosure 2.

APPENDIX B

D. POLICY

It is a DoD policy that:

1. Members of the Armed Forces shall be free to make a protected communication to a Member of Congress; an Inspector General (IG); a member of a DoD audit, inspection, investigation, or law enforcement organization; or any other person or organization (including any person or organization in the chain of command) designated under Component regulations or other established administrative procedures to receive such communications.
2. No person shall restrict a member of the Armed Forces from making a protected communication.
3. Members of the Armed Forces shall be free from reprisal for making or preparing a protected communication.
4. No person may take or threaten to take an unfavorable personnel action, or withhold or threaten to withhold a favorable personnel action, in reprisal against any member of the Armed Forces for making or preparing a protected communication.
5. Any violation of subsection D.4., above, by a person subject to Chapter 47 of 10 U.S.C. (reference (b)), is punishable as a violation of Section 892 of reference (b). Any violation of subsection D.4., above, by a civilian employee is punishable under regulations governing disciplinary adverse actions.

E. RESPONSIBILITIES

1. The Inspector General of the Department of Defense shall:
   a. Expeditiously initiate, or request the IG of a DoD Component to initiate, an investigation of an allegation submitted to the IG, DoD, by a member of the Armed Forces, that the prohibitions of subsection D.4., above, have been violated. No investigation is required when such allegation is submitted to the IG, DoD, more than 60 days after a member became aware of the personnel action that is the subject of the allegation. When the IG, DoD, requests the IG of the DoD Component to conduct the investigation, the IG, DoD, shall:

      (1) Ensure that the IG conducting the investigation is outside the immediate chain of command (as established under

Component regulations) of the member submitting the allegation and the individual(s) alleged to have taken the reprisal action.

(2) Review and determine the adequacy of the investigation. If such an investigation is inadequate, initiate a follow-up investigation to correct those inadequacies or ensure that the IG of a DoD Component corrects them.

b. Issue a report of investigation within 90 days of the receipt of the allegation of reprisal. If a determination is made that the report cannot be issued within that time, notify the Assistant Secretary of Defense for Force Management Policy (ASD(FMP)) and the member or former member of the reasons for the delay and when that report will be issued.

c. Notify the ASD(FMP)) of the results of the investigation and provide a copy of the report of investigation to the member or former member not later than 30 days after completion of the investigation. The report of investigation shall include a thorough review of the facts and circumstances relevant to the allegations, relevant documents acquired during the investigation, and summaries of interviews conducted. The report may include a recommendation as to the disposition of the complaint. The copy of the report released to the member or former member shall include the maximum disclosure of information possible except what is not required to be disclosed under 5 U.S.C. 552 (reference (d)).

d. Advise the member or former member concerned that he or she may request review of the matter by a board for correction of military records (BCMR).

e. At the request of a BCMR:

(1) Submit a copy of the report of investigation to the BCMR.
(2) Gather further evidence.

f. After the final action on a military reprisal complaint filed with the IG, DoD, when possible, interview the member or former member who made the allegation to determine his or her view on the disposition of the matter.

g. Initiate, or request the IG of a DoD Component to initiate, a separate investigation into the allegations contained in the protected communication when:

(1) Such an investigation has not already been started.
(2) The IG, DoD, determines the investigation was biased or inadequate.

h. When an investigation under paragraph E.1.g., above, is required, submit a report on the results of the investigation to the ASD(FMP) and a copy of the report of investigation to the member or former member. The report of investigation shall include a thorough review of the facts and circumstances relevant to the allegations, relevant documents acquired during the investigation, and summaries of interviews taken. The copy of the report released to the member or former member shall include the maximum disclosure of information possible except what is not required to be disclosed under Section 552 of reference (d).

2. The Assistant Secretary of Defense for Force Management Policy, under the Under Secretary of Defense for Personnel and Readiness, shall:

a. On behalf of the Secretary of Defense, within 90 days of receipt of a request submitted under enclosure 1, section C., review the final decision of the Secretary of the Military Department concerned on applications for correction of military records decided under this Directive and 10 U.S.C. 1034 (reference (b)), and decide whether to uphold or reverse the decision of the Secretary of the Military Department concerned. The decision on behalf of the Secretary of Defense is final.

b. Have access to all research, reports, investigations, audits, reviews, documents, papers, or any other material necessary to carry out the responsibilities assigned to the ASD(FMP) by this Directive.

c. If necessary, obtain for review and request the Secretary of the Military Department concerned to comment on evidence considered by a BCMR when the Secretary of Defense is requested to reconsider the final decision of the Secretary concerned.

d. Notify the IG, DoD, of decisions made for the Secretary of Defense on requests submitted under enclosure 1, section C and issue such DoD Instructions as may be necessary to implement this subsection (E.2.) and the requirements of enclosure 1, section C.

3. The Secretaries of the Military Departments and the Heads of the Other DoD Components shall:

a. Ensure that the Military Department or other Component IG (as applicable) shall:

(1) On receipt of an allegation of reprisal from a military member, advise the member in writing that to obtain consideration of the matter under this Directive, complaints of reprisal must be made to the IG, DoD, or forwarded to the IG, DoD, under enclosure 1, section A.

(2) On written request of the member, forward the allegation to the IG, DoD., under enclosure 1, section A. When an allegation of reprisal is made against a senior official of the Department of Defense, DoD Directive 5505.6 (reference (e)) also applies.

(3) At the request of the IG, DoD, investigate the allegation of reprisal and provide the IG, DoD, within 90 days of the request, the report of investigation. That report shall include a thorough review of the facts and circumstances relevant to the allegation, relevant documents acquired during the investigation, and summaries of interviews conducted. The report may include a recommendation as to the disposition of the complaint. The copy of the report submitted to the IG, DoD, for release to the member or former member shall include the maximum disclosure of information possible except what is not required to be disclosed under 5 U.S.C. 552 (reference (d)).

(4) At the request of the IG, DoD, investigate the allegations contained in the member's protected communication. The report of investigation shall include a thorough review of the facts and circumstances relevant to the allegations, relevant documents acquired during the investigation, and summaries of interviews taken. The report may include a

recommendation as to the disposition of the complaint. The copy of the report submitted to the IG, DoD, for release to the member or former member shall include the maximum disclosure of information possible except what is not required to be disclosed under Section 552 of reference (d).

b. Based on the IG report of investigation, take correction action, to include providing assistance to members preparing an application to a BCMR, when implementation of the recommendations of the report requires action by a BCMR.

c. Ensure that the subject(s) of the investigation of an allegation of reprisal conducted under this Directive are afforded procedural protections, including the opportunity to present matters in their behalf, incident to administrative or disciplinary action, under Component regulations or other established administrative procedures governing such action.

d. Publicize the content of this Directive to ensure that military and other DoD personnel fully understand its scope and application.

4. The secretaries of the Military Departments shall:

a. Ensure that the BCMR:

(1) Considers applications for the correction of military records at the request of a member or former member, or otherwise, who alleged that the prohibitions of subsection D.4., above, have been violated.

(2) In resolving such an application:

(a) Shall review the report by the IG under paragraph E.1.a., above.

(b) May request the IG, DoD, to gather further evidence.

(c) May receive oral argument, examine and cross-examine witnesses, take depositions, and, if appropriate, conduct a hearing. If a hearing is held, the requirements of enclosure 1, section B., shall apply.

(d) If the BCMR determines that a personnel action was in reprisal under this Directive, it may recommend to the Secretary of the Military Department concerned that disciplinary action be taken against the individual(s) responsible for such personnel action.

b. Issue a final decision on an application received under this Directive within 180 days after the application is filed. If the Secretary of the Military Department concerned fails to issue a final decision within that time, the member or former member shall be deemed to have exhausted the administrative remedies under 10 U.S.C. 1552 (reference (b)). Advise the member or former member that he or she may request review of the matter by the Secretary of Defense, under subsection E.2., above, and enclosure 1, section C., and that such a request must be made within 90 days of receipt of a decision by the Secretary of the Military Department concerned on the matter.

c. Order such action, consistent with the limitations in Sections 1552 and 1553 of reference (b), to correct the record of a personnel action prohibited by subsection D.4., above.

d. Notify the IG, DoD, and the Military Department or other Component IG, of a decision on an application for the correction of military records received from a member or decisions on an application for the correction of military records received from a member or former member of the Armed Forces under this Directive and of any disciplinary action taken.

F. EFFECTIVE DATE

This Directive is effective immediately.[12]

John P. White
Deputy Secretary of Defense

Enclosures—2
  1. Requirements
  2. Definitions

APPENDIX B

REQUIREMENTS

A. FILING A COMPLAINT OF REPRISAL

To be considered under this Directive, a complaint of reprisal (as defined in enclosure 2, definition 9) must be made to the IG, DoD. The member or former member may request the complaint be forwarded to the IG, DoD, by the IG of a DoD Component.

1. Time Limits. No investigation is required when a complaint is made or forwarded to the IG, DoD, more than 60 days after a member became aware of the personnel action at issue.
2. Address. Complaints of reprisal may be made by telephone to the IG, DoD, at (800) 424-9098 or by letter addressed, as follows:

> Department of Defense Inspector General
> ATTENTION: Defense Hotline
> 1900 Defense Pentagon
> Washington, DC 90301-1900

3. Content of Complaint. To assist in the review of the complaint, provide as much of the following information as possible:

    a. Member's full name, rank, duty title, organization, duty location, commercial or Defense Switches Network (DSN) telephone numbers, and residence telephone number and mailing address for receipt of correspondence from the IG, DoD.
    b. A copy of the protected communication (as defined in enclosure 2, definition 8) and any reply about the matter. If a copy is not available, include the date of the protected communication, to whom the protected communication was made, the content of the protected communication, and whether the matter was investigated, when and by whom.
    c. Identify the personnel action(s) (as defined in enclosure 2, definition 7) taken, withheld or threatened to be taken or withheld. Provide documentation about the personnel action or describe the type of personnel action and the date such action occurred.
    d. Provide to the extent possible, the full name, rank and/or grade, duty title, organization, duty location, and commercial or DSN

telephone number of the officials responsible for signing, taking recommending, or influencing the personnel action at issue. Indicate why and how any official involved in the personnel action knew of the protected communication.

e. List key witnesses and the information they have that will establish the personnel action at issue was in reprisal for making or preparing a protected communication; include commercial and DSN telephone numbers or other information on how to contact the witnesses.

f. Provide any other information in support of the allegations. If possible, provide a chronology of events, including the date of the protected communication and dates of all subsequent personnel actions taken, withheld, or threatened to be taken or withheld.

B. HEARING HELD BY A BCMR

If a BCMR elects to hold an administrative hearing under subparagraph E.4.a. (2) of the main body of this Directive, above, the member or former member who filed the application:

1. May be represented by a judge advocate if all of the following conditions exist:

   a. The IG investigation finds there is probable cause that a personnel action was in reprisal for a member of the Armed Forces making or preparing a protected communication.

   b. The Judge Advocate General concerned determines that the case is unusually complex or otherwise requires judge advocate assistance to ensure proper presentation of the legal issues in the case.

   c. The member is not represented by outside counsel retained by the member.

2. May examine witnesses through depositions, serve interrogatories, and request the production of evidence, including evidence in an IG investigatory record not included in the report released to the member or former member.

C. APPEAL TO THE SECRETARY OF DEFENSE

A member or former member of the Armed Forces who has filed an application for the correction of military records under 10 U.S.C. 1024 (reference (b)) alleging reprisal for making or preparing a protected communication may request review by the Secretary of Defense of the final decision of the Secretary of the Military Department concerned on such application under this section and subparagraph E.2.a. of the main body of this Directive, above.

1. Requests based on factual allegations or evidence not previously presented to the cognizant BCMR shall not be considered.
2. New allegations or evidence must be submitted directly to the BCMR for reconsideration under procedures established by the BCMR
3. Content of Appeal. The appeal to the Secretary of Defense must be in writing and include the following:

    a. Member's full name, rank, duty title, organization, duty location, and commercial or DSN telephone numbers.
    b. A copy of the application to the BCMR and the final decision by or for the Secretary of the Military Department concerned on such application.
    c. A statement of the specific reasons why the member or former member is not satisfied with the decision of the Secretary of the Military Department concerned and the specific remedy or relief requested.

4. Time Limits. The request for review by the Secretary of Defense must be submitted within 90 days of receipt of the final decision by or for the Secretary of the Military Department concerned.
5. Address. Address requests for review by the Secretary of Defense as follows:

Assistant Secretary of Defense
for Force Management Policy
Attention: Director, Legal Policy
4000 Defense Pentagon
Washington, DC 20301-4000

DEFINITIONS

1. Audit, Inspection, Investigation, and Law Enforcement Organizations. The law enforcement organizations at any command level in any of the DoD Components, the Defense Criminal Investigative Service, the U.S. Army Criminal Investigation Command, the Naval Criminal Investigative Service, the Air Force Office of Special Investigations, the U.S. Army Audit Agency, the Naval Audit Service, the Air Force Audit Agency, and the Defense Contract Audit Agency.

2. Board for Correction of Military Records (BCMR). Any board empowered under 10 U.S.C. 1552 (reference (b)) to recommend correction of military records to the Secretary of the Military Department concerned.

3. Corrective Action. Any action deemed necessary to make the complainant whole; changes in Agency regulations or practices; administrative or disciplinary action against offending personnel; or referral to the U.S. Attorney General or court-martial convening authority of any evidence of criminal violation.

4. Inspector General (IG). An IG appointed under Appendix III of 5 U.S.C. (reference (d)); or an officer of the Armed Forces or civilian employee assigned, detailed, or employed as an IG at any command level in one of the DoD Components.

5. Member of Congress. Besides a Senator or Representative, includes any Delegate or Resident Commissioner to the Congress.

6. Member or Member of the Armed Forces. All Regular and Reserve component officers (commissioned and warrant) and enlisted members of the Army, the Navy, the Air Force, the Marine Corps, and the Coast Guard (when it is operating as a Military Service in the Navy) on active duty, and Reserve component officers (commissioned and warrant) and enlisted members in any duty or training status. Includes professors and cadets of the Military Service academies and officers and enlisted members of the National Guard.

7. Personnel Action. Any action taken on a member of the Armed Forces that affects or has the potential to affect that military member's current position or career. Such actions include a promotion; a disciplinary or other corrective action; a transfer or reassignment; a performance evaluation; a decision on pay, benefits, awards, or training; referral for mental health evaluations under DoD Directive 6490.1 (reference (c)); and any other significant change in duties or responsibilities inconsistent with the military member's rank.

8. Protected Communication
   a. Any lawful communication to a Member of Congress or an IG.
   b. A communication in which a member of the Armed Forces communicates information that the member reasonably believes evidences a violation of law or regulation, including sexual harassment or unlawful discrimination, mismanagement, a gross waste of funds or other resources, an abuse of authority, or a substantial and specific danger to public health or safety, WHEN such communication is made to any of the following:[13]

   (1) A member of Congress, an IG, or a member of a DoD audit, inspection, investigation, or law enforcement organization.
   (2) Any other person or organization (including any person or Organization in the chain of command) designated under Component regulations or other established administrative procedures to receive such communications.

9. Reprisal. Taking or threatening to take an unfavorable personnel action, or withholding or threatening to withhold a favorable personnel action, for making or preparing a protected communication.
10. Senior Official. Active duty, retired, Reserve, or National Guard military officers in grades O-7 and above, current and former civilians in the grade of GS or GM-16 or above, current or former members of the Senior Executive Service, and current and former DoD civilian presidential appointees.
11. Unlawful Discrimination. Discrimination on the basis of color, national origin, race, religion or sex, as set forth in 10 U.S.C. 1034 (reference (b)).
12. Whistleblower. A member of the Armed Forces who makes or prepares to make a protected communication.

ENDNOTES

1. 1 Peter 3:17
2. Mental Health Evaluation of Members of the Armed Forces (See Appendix A)
3. Psalm 25:2 (NASB emphasis added)
4. Psalm 10:12–13,15
5. Psalm 11:6–7
6. From "A Compilation of Physician's Oaths," Charles S. Yanofsky, M.D., 2004. susqneuro.com/publications/oaths/index.html.
7. John 3:19
8. The Book of Job in the Bible tells of a righteous man named Job who suffered at the hands of the devil.
9. Ephesians 2:2 (KJV)
10. *The Moving Finger*, Agatha Christie, (New York: Berkley Books, 1984), p. 198
11. Pronounced "Mee-lie." Refers to a massacre of a Vietnamese village by US troops on March 16, 1968.
12. As required by Section 1034 of reference (b), any implementing documents must stipulate that a violation of the prohibition in subsection D.F., above, by a person subject to Chapter 47 of reference (b), is punishable as a violation of Section 892 of reference (b), and that such a violation by a DoD civilian employee is punishable under regulations governing disciplinary or adverse action.
13. DoD Directive 7050.1 (reference (f)), further defines applicable terms.

Made in the USA
Monee, IL
25 November 2020